A Concise
Introduction
to Islam

by
Jerald F. Dirks

amana publications

First Edition
(1435 AH/2014 AC)

Copyright © 1435 AH/2014 AC
amana publications
10710 Tucker Street
Beltsville, MD 20705-2223 USA
Tel. 301.595.5777
Fax 301.595.5888, 240.250.3000
Email: amana@igprinting.com
        amana@amana-corp.com
Website: www.amana-publications.com

Library of Congress Cataloging-in-Publication Data

Dirks, Jerald.
 A concise introduction to islam / by Jerald F. Dirks.
     pages cm
 Includes bibliographical references.
 ISBN 978-1-59008-080-1 (alk. paper)
 1. Islam. I. Title.
 BP161.3.D569 2014
 297--dc23
                        2014017454

Table of Contents

~

~

Chapter One

FINDING COMMON GROUND

INTRODUCTION

Suicide bombings of innocent and unarmed civilians in Israel/Palestine... Quasi-public strip searches of Palestinian women by male Israeli soldiers... Fuel-laden airplanes crashing into the World Trade Center... An Armageddon in which Jews and Muslims are wiped from the face of the earth and only Christians of a certain persuasion are left... If one were to believe the subtle suggestions of our morning newspapers and evening news shows and the blatant pronouncements of some well-known ministers of the extreme Christian Right, one would have to conclude that we are standing at the dawn of a massive clash of religious civilizations, a cataclysmic war of the religious worlds.

Why? Can three so closely interrelated religions that share so much common ground be inevitably destined to endless confrontation and mutual vilification? Perhaps the problem is that the adherents of Judaism, Christianity, and Islam fail to realize that the differences that divide them cover a relatively small terrain compared to the tremendous common ground they share. As such, I'd like to plow a few acres of that expansive common ground and thereby suggest that the proper mode of interaction among Judaism, Christianity, and Islam is cooperation, not confrontation.

However, before beginning our journey into the common ground that is Judaism, Christianity, and Islam, I should note two things. Firstly, it is customary for Muslims to say, "Peace be upon him," after mentioning one of the prophets. Muslims also typically use the Arabic word "Allah" instead of the English word "God." For your ease of reading, I am abandoning both of those conventions in this brief introduction to Islam.

PLACING THE ABRAHAMIC FAITHS IN CONTEXT

Perhaps we can begin our journey into common ground with the academic discipline of comparative religion. The study of comparative religion offers a variety of ways to classify the various religions of the world: monotheistic vs. polytheistic, prophetic tradition vs. wisdom tradition, and Middle Eastern vs. Eastern. Within the context of the major world religions, the three great monotheistic religions are Judaism, Christianity, and Islam. The three major prophetic religions are Judaism, Christianity, and Islam, and the three primary Middle Eastern religions are Judaism, Christianity, and Islam. More specifically, these three religions are often classified together as the three Abrahamic faiths.

It's no accident that these three religions consistently group together across a variety of conceptual schemata. While each of the three religions has dogma and doctrine unique to itself, each of them has a core that is essentially similar to the core of the other two. Each of the three religions claims the same historical legacy within the prophetic tradition, although each may interpret specific historical and prophetic events somewhat differently. Using the analogy of a tree, each of the three religions claims to be the one, true, vertical extension of a trunk of primary revelation, with the other two religions being seen as lateral branches that deviate somewhat from the true verticality of the original trunk.

COMMON GROUND: THE PROPHETIC TRADITION

THE OLD TESTAMENT PROPHETS

In exploring the common ground to be found among the three Abrahamic faiths, I have already alluded to their shared prophetic tradition. The prophetic tradition within Judaism and Christianity is firmly encapsulated in what Christianity refers to as the Old Testament. Moving from Genesis to Malachi, Judaism and Christianity trace their prophetic tradition from the creation of Adam, through the pre-Israelite patriarchs (Noah, Enoch, Abraham, Ishmael, and Isaac), and on through various Israelite prophets and notables (Jacob, Joseph, Moses, Samuel, David, Solomon, Elijah, Elisha, Jonah, etc.). Within Christianity, the prophetic tradition even encroaches slightly into the New Testament gospels, with stories about Zechariah and his son, John the Baptist.

It may come as a surprise to some readers to learn that everyone of these aforementioned prophets and notables is mentioned repeatedly in the Qur'an, Islam's book of Holy Scripture. Utilizing a standard English translation of the meaning of the Qur'an, one finds Moses being named over 170 times, Abraham over 70 times, Noah over 40 times, Jesus and Joseph (the son of Jacob) over 30 times, Adam, Jacob, and King Solomon almost 20 times, Isaac and King David over 15 times, and John the Baptist about five times. Within the Qur'an, one also finds references to Job, Samuel, Jonah, Elijah, and Elisha. Clearly, this is a shared prophetic tradition among Judaism, Christianity, and Islam.

When one compares the stories of the prophets mentioned in both the Bible and the Qur'an, one typically finds that the two sources parallel each other, although occasionally disagreeing about some specific details of the story. This is the case with such stories as Adam's creation and fall, Noah and the flood, Abraham's trial by being asked to sacrifice his son, Joseph being sold into slavery and later becoming the vizier of Egypt, the infant Moses being cast out on the water by his mother and later leading the Israelites out of Egypt, Jonah being swallowed by a big fish, the miraculous birth of John the Baptist, etc. In addition, one often finds that the respective stories of

5

the prophets from the *Bible* and the *Qur'an* tend to complement each other without overlapping. Thus, the *Qur'an* gives considerable detail about Abraham's early life, presumably in Ur. While such information is not to be found in the *Bible*, it does not contradict Biblical accounts and often has parallel accounts in the Jewish *Talmud*. In contrast, the *Bible* gives information about Abraham's life in Palestine that is not to be found in the *Qur'an* but that does not contradict the *Qur'an*.

True, there are places where the Judaeo-Christian and Islamic traditions differ. While both traditions maintain that God created the universe in six units of time, the *Qur'an* offers no parallel to the Biblical account of God resting from His work on the seventh day. While both traditions maintain that Adam fell from grace by eating of the forbidden fruit in the garden, Islam and Judaism, unlike traditional Western Christianity, do not interpret this fall as creating a state of Original Sin, in which all of humanity somehow inherits Adam's initial sin. While both traditions maintain that Abraham was called upon to offer his son in sacrifice, the Judaeo-Christian tradition maintains that the sacrificial victim was Isaac, while the Islamic tradition usually holds that it was Ishmael.

JESUS AND MARY

Both Islam and Christianity proclaim the virgin birth of Jesus. However, there is a fundamental difference between the two religions in terms of how the virgin birth is typically conceptualized. Christianity usually portrays the virgin birth of Jesus in terms of his being the "begotten" son of God. For example, Matthew 1:18 states that Mary was "with child from the Holy Spirit." In contrast, Islam's portrayal of the virgin birth is that of a miraculous creation, not that of divine begetting.

> "But my Lord!" She [Mary] cried out. "How can I have a son when no man has touched me?" "And so it is that God creates whatever He wants," the angels replied. "When He decides something, He only has to say, 'Be,' and it is."...The example of Jesus in the sight of God is like that of Adam. He created him from dust, saying, "Be," and he was. (*Qur'an* 3:47, 59)

While many passages in the *Qur'an* deal with the mission, ministry, and miracles of Jesus, *Qur'an* 3:49 provides the most succinct encapsulation. This single verse informs the reader that Jesus performed many miracles "by God's command" (e.g., turning a clay figure of a bird into a living bird, healing the blind and the lepers, and reviving the dead) and that he declared "what you consume (and waste of the world), as well as what you store away (of good deeds for Judgment Day)." In addition, *Qur'an* 19:27-34 states that Jesus spoke during infancy, and *Qur'an* 5:46 reports that God gave Jesus a gospel "in which there was both guidance and enlightenment, as an affirmation of the Torah that had come before him."

Now, the story of the clay birds and of Jesus speaking in infancy may be new to most Christians, but both stories appear in early Christian literature. The First Gospel of the Infancy of Jesus Christ 1:2 details Jesus speaking in infancy, while 15:6 of the same apocryphal gospel and 1:2-10 of Thomas' Gospel of the Infancy of Jesus Christ narrate the story of the clay birds coming to life. Further, the list of miracles given in *Qur'an* 3:49 appears to overlap quite comfortably with similar lists given in the New Testament gospels. For example, the *Qur'an* has Jesus saying:

> ...I'll heal the blind and the lepers and bring the dead to life, all by God's command. I'll tell you what you consume (and waste of the world), as well as what you store away (of good deeds for Judgment Day). (Know that) in all of these things is a great sign if you really have faith. (*Qur'an* 3:49)

Similarly, the New Testament gospels have Jesus saying:

> ...Go and tell John what you have seen and heard: the blind receive their sight, the lame walk, the lepers are cleansed, the deaf hear, the dead are raised, the poor have good news brought to them... (Luke 7:22)

Finally, Islam, like Christianity, maintains that there is yet a future role for Jesus prior to the Day of Judgment. Similar to Christian thought, numerous sayings of Prophet Muhammad (as recorded in *Muslim* #293, 6931-6934, 7015, 7023; *Abu Dawud* #4310; and *Al-Bukhari* #3:425, 656; 4:657-658) contribute to the Islamic belief that Jesus will descend back to earth, slay the Antichrist, and establish an Earthly rule.

There is a particularly dramatic Old Testament passage that many Christians interpret as referring to this coming Messianic reign. It is striking for its contrasts and juxtapositions.

> The wolf shall live with the lamb, the leopard shall lie down with the kid, the calf and the lion and the fatling together, and a little child shall lead them. The cow and the bear shall graze, their young shall lie down together; and the lion shall eat straw like the ox. The nursing child shall play over the hole of the asp, and the weaned child shall put its hand on the adder's den. (Isaiah 11:6-8)

The Messianic reign is described in remarkably similar terms in the following saying of Prophet Muhammad.

> During Jesus' reign, such security will exist that a camel will graze with the lion and the beast of prey with cows and sheep. Children will play with snakes, and none harm the other. (*Musnad of Ahmad ibn Hanbal*, 406:2)

COMMON GROUND: ETHICAL AND SPIRITUAL TEACHING

So far, we have been confining our exploration of the three Abrahamic faiths to the domain of the prophetic tradition. However, it is equally profitable to consider the realm of ethics and spiritual instruction.

MONOTHEISM

A central tenet of Judaism is the concept of the Unity or Oneness of God. This is succinctly expressed in the following verse, which is known as the *Shema*.

Hear O Israel, the Lord our God, the Lord is One. (Deuteronomy 6:4)

According to the New Testament, Jesus quoted these very words of the *Shema* when he was asked about the greatest of all commandments.

One of the scribes came near and heard them disputing with one another, and seeing that he answered them well, he asked him, "Which commandment is the first of all?" Jesus answered, "The first is, 'Hear, O Israel: the Lord our God, the Lord is one...'" (Mark 12:28-29)

The Unity of God is also repeatedly emphasized in the *Qur'an*. The following represent just a couple of those verses.

Your God is One God; there is no god but He, the Compassionate, the Merciful. (*Qur'an* 2:163)

Say (to them), "He is only one God." (*Qur'an* 112:1)

THE DECALOGUE

All three Abrahamic faiths stress that proper adherence to the divine revelation involves establishing a proper relationship with God and with one's fellow man. One of the first classical expressions of this viewpoint can be found in the Biblical Ten Commandments, as stated in Exodus 20:1-17 and Deuteronomy 5:1-22. Using the traditional Protestant method of counting them, these commandments may be summarized as: (1) you shall have no other gods before God; (2) you shall not make any graven images or idols; (3) you shall not take the name of the Lord, your God, in vain; (4) remember the Sabbath day, and keep it holy; (5) honor your father and your mother; (6) you shall not murder; (7) you shall not commit adultery; (8) you shall not steal; (9) you shall not bear false witness; and (10) you shall not covet. These Ten Commandments serve as a basic underpinning of the Judaeo-Christian system of ethics, and they are reflected quite dramatically in the ethical teachings of the *Qur'an*.

Your Lord has decided that you must serve no one else but Him and that you should be kind to your parents. Whether one or both of them becomes old in your lifetime, never speak to them disrespectfully nor scold them, but rather speak to them in generous terms...Don't go anywhere near any unlawful sexual activity for it's a shameful practice and opens the way (to even greater sins and dangers). Don't take the life of anyone (whose life) God has forbidden (to be taken), except for a just cause (under the law)...Give full measure (to your customers) when you measure (for them), and weigh with an accurate scale, for that's best for achieving a good result...Don't be jealous of (the material) things, (such as money or fame,) that God has blessed some of you with more than others... (*Qur'an* 17:23, 32-33a, 35; 4:32a)

Let's pause for a moment to consider these Qur'anic injunctions. (1) "Your Lord has decided that you must serve no one else but Him..." = you shall have no other gods before God. (2) "...be kind to your parents. Whether one or both of them becomes old in your lifetime, never speak to them disrespectfully nor scold them, but rather speak to them in generous terms..." = honor your father and your mother. (3) "Don't go anywhere near any unlawful sexual activity..." = you shall not commit adultery. (4) "Don't take the life of anyone (whose life) God has forbidden (to be taken), except for a just cause (under the law)..." = you shall not murder. (5) "Give full measure (to your customers) when you measure (for them), and weigh with an accurate scale..." = you shall not steal. (6) "Don't be jealous of (the material) things, (such as money or fame,) that God has blessed some of you with more than others..." = you shall not covet.

As to the remaining four moral injunctions of the Ten Commandments, one can easily find Qur'anic parallels to three of them. You shall not make any graven images or idols is consistent with Islam's traditional avoidance of creating artistic likenesses of any living creature and with the following Qur'anic injunction.

...shun the abomination of idols... (*Qur'an* 22:30)

You shall not take the name of the Lord, your God, in vain is paralleled by *Qur'an* 2:224 and 24:53.

Don't take the name of God as an excuse if the promise is against doing good, acting rightly or making peace among people, for God hears and knows (what you're doing). (*Qur'an* 2:224)

(The hypocrites) swear to God adamantly, claiming that if you but gave the command, they would leave (their homes and march with the militia in times of war). Tell them,

9

"Don't just swear on it, for actual obedience is a more fitting (way to prove your sincerity), and God is well-informed about what you're doing." (*Qur'an* 24:53)

You shall not bear false witness finds expression in many passages of the *Qur'an* (e.g., 2:42; 4:112; 25:72-75; 40:28; 45:27; 51:10; 56:92; and 58:14-15) but is perhaps expressed best in the following verse.

Don't confuse the truth with falsehood, nor conceal the truth knowingly. (*Qur'an* 2:42)

Thus, only the Decalogue's injunction to remember the Sabbath day is not to be found in Islam.

THE SACREDNESS OF LIFE

The sacredness of life that is implied in the Decalogue's "thou shalt not murder" is dramatically reinforced in the Jewish *Babylonian Talmud*.

...whoever destroys a single Israelite soul is deemed by scripture as if he had destroyed a whole world. And whoever saves a single Israelite soul is deemed by scripture as if he had saved a whole world. (Tractate Sanhedrin 4:5, J-K)

The *Qur'an* echoes this statement from the *Babylonian Talmud*, but makes it a much broader statement, one that stresses the sacredness of all human life, not just Israelite life.

....We made it a principle for the Children of Israel that if anyone took a life, unless it be (to punish) a murder or to prevent the spread of chaos in the land, that it would be as if he had murdered the whole of humanity. (*Qur'an* 5:32)

THE *LEX TALIONIS*

Another fundamental ethical precept of the Old Testament is the *Lex Talionis* (law of retaliation in kind) found in the so-called Mosaic Law.

If any harm follows, then you shall give life for life, eye for eye, tooth for tooth, hand for hand, foot for foot, burn for burn, wound for wound, stripe for stripe. (Exodus 21:23-25)

Of note, the New Testament claims that Jesus modified this Lex Talionis when he reportedly said:

You have heard that it was said, "An eye for an eye and a tooth for a tooth." But I say to you, do not resist an evildoer. But if anyone strikes you on the right cheek, turn the other also; and if anyone wants to sue you and take your coat, give your cloak as well; and if anyone forces you to go one mile, go also the second mile. (Matthew 5:38-41)

In the above verses, Jesus reportedly suggests that the *Lex Talionis* should be softened with charity, mercy, and forgiveness. This call for a compassionate modification of the *Lex Talionis* is also found in the *Qur'an*.

> We decreed for them in (the Torah): "A life for a life, an eye for an eye, a nose for a nose, an ear for an ear, a tooth for a tooth, and a wound in exchange for a wound." Now (this principle has been amended,) so if anyone chooses to refrain from retaliating, for (the sake of charity), then it's an act of atonement for himself. (*Qur'an* 5:45)

> Goodness and evil are not equal, so ward off (evil) by doing good. That's how you can turn your enemy into your close supporter and ally. (*Qur'an* 41:34)

SOCIAL DUTY

Let us consider another of the great ethical teachings attributed to Jesus in the New Testament, one that dramatically illustrates our social duty and responsibility to our fellow man.

> Then he will say to those at his left hand, "You that are accursed, depart from me into the eternal fire prepared for the devil and his angels; for I was hungry and you gave me no food, I was thirsty and you gave me nothing to drink, I was a stranger and you did not welcome me, naked and you did not give me clothing, sick and in prison and you did not visit me." Then they also will answer, "Lord, when was it that we saw you hungry or thirsty or a stranger or naked or sick or in prison, and did not take care of you?" Then he will answer them, "Truly I tell you, just as you did not do it to one of the least of these, you did not do it to me." And these will go away into eternal punishment, but the righteous into eternal life. (Matthew 25:41-46)

Islam offers an almost identical ethical instruction, which is found in the sayings of Prophet Muhammad.

> God's Messenger said: "Verily, God, the exalted and glorious, will say on the Day of Resurrection: 'O son of Adam, I was sick but you did not visit Me.' He will say: 'O my Lord, how could I visit You when You are the Lord of the worlds?' Thereupon He will say: 'Didn't you know that a certain servant of Mine was sick, but you did not visit him, and were you not aware that if you had visited him, you would have found Me by him? O son of Adam, I asked you for food but you did not feed Me.' He will say: 'My Lord, how could I feed You when You are the Lord of the worlds?' He will say: 'Didn't you know that a certain servant of Mine asked you for food but you did not feed him, and were

you not aware that if you had fed him you would have found him by My side?' (The Lord will again say:) 'O son of Adam, I asked you for something to drink, but you did not provide Me with any.' He will say: 'My Lord, how could I provide You with something to drink when You are the Lord of the worlds?' Thereupon, He will say: 'A certain servant of Mine asked you for a drink but you did not provide him with one, and had you provided him with a drink you would have found him near Me.'" (*Muslim, Hadith* #6232)

FALSE PIETY IN CHARITY

In another passage, the New Testament reports that Jesus warned his followers against false piety in giving alms, stressed that one's heavenly reward is based upon one's intentions as much as one's behavior, and suggested that one's acts of charity should not be made public.

Beware of practicing your piety before others in order to be seen by them; for then you have no reward from your Father in heaven. So whenever you give alms, do not sound a trumpet before you, as the hypocrites do in the synagogues and in the streets, so that they may be praised by others. Truly I tell you, they have received their reward. But when you give alms, do not let your left hand know what your right hand is doing, so that your alms may be done in secret; and your Father who sees in secret will reward you. (Matthew 6:1-4)

The following passage from the *Qur'an* appears to be a direct parallel.

All you who believe! Don't negate your charity by making others feel they owe you or by humiliating (the poor). This is what the boastful do when they spend to be seen by other people, for they don't really believe in God and the Last Day. (*Qur'an* 2:264a)

Before leaving our consideration of Matthew 6:1-4, it may be helpful to quote an example from the sayings of Prophet Muhammad, one that parallels the reported words of Jesus regarding the proper way of giving alms.

God's Messenger said: "When God created the earth...the angels...asked if anything in His creation was stronger than wind, and He replied, 'Yes, the son of Adam who gives charity with his right hand while concealing it from his left.'" (*Al-Tirmidhi, Hadith* #192)

FALSE PIETY IN PRAYER

The New Testament states that Jesus also warned against false piety in the performance of prayers.

And whenever you pray, do not be like the hypocrites; for they love to stand and pray in the synagogues and at the street corners, so that they may be seen by others. Truly I tell you, they have received their reward. (Matthew 6:5)

Similar sentiments are expressed in the *Qur'an*.

So a warning to those who pray—to those who are careless in their devotions, whose prayers are only for show, and yet who refuse to share even the smallest of favors. (*Qur'an* 107:4-7)

In closing its discussion of false piety in prayer, the New Testament states that Jesus reportedly said:

When you are praying, do not heap up empty phrases as the Gentiles do; for they think that they will be heard because of their many words. (Matthew 6:7)

The ethical considerations stated in Matthew 6:7 find clear and unambiguous expression in a saying of Prophet Muhammad, wherein he implied that the Antichrist was less of a threat to a believer, than was the believer who altered his prayer out of false piety.

God's Messenger came out to them when they were discussing the Antichrist and asked if they would like him to tell what caused him more fear for them than the Antichrist. They replied that they certainly would, so he said, "Latent polytheism, meaning that a man will stand up and pray and lengthen his prayer because he sees someone looking at him." (*Al-Tirmidhi, Hadith* #5333)

THE GOLDEN RULE:

For many Christians, the pinnacle of the reported ethical instruction of Jesus can be found in the so-called Golden Rule.

In everything do to others as you would have them do to you; for this is the law and the prophets. (Matthew 7:12)

Variations on the Golden Rule can also be found in prior Jewish writings. For example, a precursor to the Golden Rule is attributed to Rabbi Hillel, in which he instructed that one should not do to others what one would not want done to oneself. An additional Jewish precursor to the Golden Rule can be identified in the Old Testament Apocrypha.

And what you hate, do to no man. (Tobit 4:14)

The Islamic parallel to the Golden Rule can be found in the teachings of Prophet Muhammad.

The Prophet said: "None of you will have faith till he wishes for his brother what he likes for himself." (*Al-Bukhari*, volume 1, *Hadith* #12)

DRAWING NEAR TO GOD

The New Testament's Epistle of James states that if a person will only come close to God, God will come close to him.

Draw near to God, and he will draw near to you. (James 4:8)

In a much more dramatic manner, similar sentiments are expressed in the following statement of Prophet Muhammad.

The Prophet said, "God says...'I am with him (man) if he remembers Me. If he remembers Me in himself, I too, remember him in Myself; and if he remembers Me in a group of people, I remember him in a group that is better than they; and if he comes one span (about eight to nine inches) nearer to Me, I go one cubit (about 18-20 inches) nearer to him; and if he comes one cubit nearer to Me, I go a distance of two outstretched arms nearer to him; and if he comes to Me walking, I go to him running.'" (*Al-Bukhari*, volume #9, *Hadith* #502)

GOD WILLING:

Consider one final example of the commonality to be found between Islam and the Judaeo-Christian tradition. The New Testament author of the Epistle of James warns man against taking himself too seriously.

Come now, you who say, "Today or tomorrow we will go to such and such a town and spend a year there, doing business and making money." Yet you do not even know what tomorrow will bring. What is your life? For you are a mist that appears for a little while and then vanishes. Instead you ought to say, "If the Lord wishes, we will live and do this or that." As it is, you boast in your arrogance; all such boasting is evil. (James 4:13-16)

The *Qur'an* also warns against this type of arrogance.

Never say of anything, "I'll do it tomorrow," without adding, "If God wills." (*Qur'an* 18:23-24a)

DIFFERENCES AMONG THE ABRAHAMIC FAITHS

All of the above is not to say that there are no differences among the three Abrahamic faiths. The differences among Judaism, Christianity, and Islam are very real, are important and fundamental, and will be explored in chapter IV. At this time, it is sufficient to note that among these fundamental differences that divide the Abrahamic faiths, one can list the following issues: (1) the divine mission and ministry of Jesus Christ—universal according to contemporary Christianity, specific to the children of Israel according to Islam and several branches of ancient Christianity, and non-existent according to traditional Judaism; (2) the alleged crucifixion of Jesus—reality according to contemporary Christianity, fiction according to Islam and several branches of ancient Christianity; (3) the nature of Jesus—combined humanity and divinity according to contemporary Christianity, humanity according to Islam, Judaism, and several branches of ancient Christianity; and (4) the nature of God—trinity according to contemporary Christianity, unity according to Islam, Judaism, and several branches of ancient Christianity. Additional disagreements among the Abrahamic faiths concern the status of Muhammad as a prophet of God, the status of the contemporary *Bible* as divine revelation, and the status of the *Qur'an* as divine revelation.

These differences should not be swept under the proverbial rug, simply in order to rush forward to an ecumenical embrace among the three Abrahamic faiths. We need to acknowledge honestly and discuss openly those differences. In doing so, our goal must be to seek mutual understanding, if not theological agreement. Moreover, our religious differences should not obscure our equally real and equally important similarities in religious history, heritage, and core beliefs. Nor should these differences blind us to the fact that we, as Jews, Christians, and Muslims, share a common core of ethical values, a common embrace of spiritual idealism, and a common religious belief in our social obligations and duties to our fellow man.

Chapter Two

CLEARING UP MISCONCEPTIONS

INTRODUCTION

Misconceptions about and misrepresentations of Islam are far too common in the Western world. The professional media, the internet, unsolicited e-mails, and religious demagoguery all play their part in promoting these misconceptions. In what follows, some of the more common misconceptions about Islam are examined.

COMMON MISCONCEPTIONS INVOLVING ARABIC WORDS

THE ARABIC WORD "ALLAH"

The Arabic word "Allah" often raises the specter of some cult deity to Americans. Some proponents of the extreme Christian Right even make the specious claim that Allah is nothing more than an Arab moon god. In reality, the Arabic word "Allah" is merely a contraction of the Arabic "Al-Ilah," which literally means "the God" and, at least by implication, "the One God." Further, Arabic and Hebrew are sister languages among the Semitic language group, and the Arabic "Al-Ilah" is linguistically comparable to the Hebrew "Elohim" and "El-Elohim," which are the Hebrew words that are typically translated as "God" in most English versions of the Old Testament. Whether one says God, Allah, or *Elohim*, the intended meaning is the same.

We can draw that connection between "*Al-Ilah*" and "*El-Elohim*" even closer by looking at the spellings of both. Remembering that neither Arabic nor Hebrew has vowels, the spelling of "*Al-Ilah*" in Arabic letters is "*Alif-Lam-Alif-Lam-Ha*." Now let's consider "*El-Elohim*," which is spelled in Hebrew letters as "*Alif-Lam-Alif-Lam-Ha-Yod-Mim*." The only difference between the two is that the Hebrew adds a "*Yod*" and a "*Mim*" to the end, with those additional letters merely rendering the word a plural of respect—sort of like the "royal we." Otherwise, "*Al-Ilah*" and "*El-Elohim*" are identical.

ISLAM

"Islam" is an Arabic word that literally means "submission," i.e., submission to the will and pleasure of God. While "submission" is the primary definition associated with the word "Islam," there is a secondary definition, which is "peace." Thus, Islam is the religion of submission to God, and it is through this submission that one finds spiritual peace. Of note, there is no such religion as "Muhammadanism;" the name of the religion is Islam. Muslims, the adherents to Islam, vigorously object to the term "Muhammadanism," since they do not worship and do not ascribe any divinity to Prophet Muhammad.

MUSLIM

The believer in and practitioner of Islam is known as a Muslim. The words "Muslim" and "Islam" derive from the same Arabic root word, and "Muslim" literally means "one who submits," i.e., one who wholly submits to God. The follower of Islam is a Muslim, not a "Muhammadan!"

HADITH

"*Hadith*" means "narration," and its plural form is *Ahadith*. Within a religious context, a *Hadith* is a narration about what Prophet Muhammad said and did. As the *Qur'an* specifies that Prophet Muhammad is a religious example to follow, authentic *Ahadith* serve Muslims as a supplemental religious authority to the *Qur'an*. More about the *Ahadith* will be found in chapter III.

OTHER COMMON MISCONCEPTIONS

INTERRELATIONSHIP AMONG THE ABRAHAMIC FAITHS:

With regard to the interrelationship among the three Abrahamic faiths, adherents to the Judaeo-Christian tradition have been taught that Judaism was the first monotheistic religion, that Christianity was a derivation from Judaism, and that Islam was a derivation from both Judaism and Christianity. In reality, these teachings are not facts derived from religious history, but are a Judaeo-Christian interpretation of religious history, an interpretation that sees the Biblical prophets as calling the Israelites back to Judaism. The Islamic interpretation of the same historical facts is that Islam began with Adam and then progressively evolved in the prophetic tradition through successive and progressive revelations. As the centuries passed after Adam, deviations occurred in the true revelation of Islam. Despite additional prophets being sent to call the people back to Islam, some of these religious deviations became codified. Such codifications were the origins of Judaism and Christianity, with Judaism being codified primarily under the influence of Ezra and the Men of the Great Assembly circa 400 BCE, and with Christianity, at least how it has evolved into modern times, being codified primarily under the teachings of Paul (Saul of Tarsus).

MISLEADING COMPARISONS

Most non-Muslims erroneously assume that Christianity and Islam can be compared by contrasting the role of Jesus in Christianity with the role of Muhammad in Islam. An equally inappropriate comparison is to contrast the role of the *Bible* in Christianity with the role of the *Qur'an* in Islam. Much better, although by no means perfect, comparisons have been offered by the late Wilfred Cantwell Smith, a renowned professor of comparative religion.

Smith argued quite cogently in his *Islam in Modern History* that the most frequent error in contrasting Islam and Christianity is to hypothesize a comparison between the roles of Jesus in Christianity and Prophet Muhammad in Islam. Smith argued that it is more realistic and profitable to contrast Prophet Muhammad's role in Islam with the role of Paul in Christianity. Both have been referred to as apostles who preached a message whose followers believed was of divine origin. Paul's message and the message of Pauline Christianity was the very person of Jesus Christ, whom Christians frequently call the "word of God" and whom Christians typically believe to be the revelation from God—"And the Word became flesh and lived among us..." (John 1:14a). In contrast, Muslims believe that Prophet Muhammad preached the message of the *Qur'an*, i.e., the literal words of God. Thus, the role of Prophet Muhammad in Islam can be compared with the role of Paul in Christianity, and the role and status of the *Qur'an* in Islam can be contrasted with the position of Jesus Christ in Pauline Christianity.

Extending Smith's argument further, the *Bible*, i.e., contemporary Christianity's record about the revelation which was Jesus, should not be compared to the *Qur'an*, i.e., Islam's actual and verbatim revelation from God, but perhaps to the *Ahadith*, which are narratives regarding what Prophet Muhammad said and did, and which contain information regarding the history and context regarding the divine revelation to Prophet Muhammad. As such, Smith argued that within Islam, there is no Qur'anic field of study comparable to Christianity's academic and theological interest in Biblical criticism. The comparison to Biblical criticism within Christianity would be *Hadith* criticism within Islam, a field of study that is still somewhat in its early stages compared to the text critical and literary form critical studies that have been undertaken on the *Bible*. Given this presentation, perhaps the Christian can understand that asking a Muslim "for historical criticism of the *Qur'an*" is comparable, Smith says, to asking a devout Christian "for a psychoanalysis of Jesus."

MUHAMMAD IS NOT THE FOUNDER OF ISLAM

A common misconception is that Prophet Muhammad was the founder of Islam. To correct this misunderstanding, it is helpful to digress for a moment and consider the Islamic view of the concept of revelation. Islam views the prophetic tradition as being a series of progressive revelations, with each prophet being given a divine covenant. As the sequence of prophets unfolded over time and across different ethnic groups, successive revelations would sometimes add to or abrogate prior revelations. Thus, the totality of the revelation given to Moses might be somewhat different than that previously given to Abraham, that of Jesus different than that of Moses, and that of Muhammad different than that of Jesus. From an Islamic perspective, this evolution in the revelatory message indicates a gradual unfolding of God's divine plan and message, with specific changes paced to the spiritual development of humanity or to that of a specific group of people. However, throughout all of the progressive revelations given to successive prophets, Islam maintains that two core elements of the revelations remained constant. Firstly, there is no god but God, Who alone is to be worshiped in His Oneness. Secondly, avoid evil and wickedness, for there will be a general resurrection and a Day of Judgment.

Given the above, it can be seen that Muslims hold that Islam actually began with Adam, the first human. Over time, this initial Islam evolved through progressive revelation, reaching its culmination and perfect form in the revelations given to Prophet Muhammad. Prophet Muhammad was not the founder of Islam; instead, he was the last in a series of prophets who expounded Islam.

FREEDOM OF RELIGION

A common myth is that Islam forces non-Muslims to convert to Islam and to adhere to Islamic religious law. Nothing can be further from the truth. In fact, Islam expressly forbids coercion in religious belief and practice, as the following verse from the Qur'an illustrates.

There is no (permission) to force (anyone into following this) way of life. (Qur'an 2:256)

If the above statement were not definitive enough, the following verses from the Qur'an clearly state that not even Prophet Muhammad was allowed to force non-Muslims to become Muslims or to make them adhere to Islamic religious practices and conventions.

He was only allowed to "remind with this Qur'an," and "to convey (the message) clearly." He was not allowed to force anyone to convert to Islam, and neither is any Muslim allowed to do so.

> If God had wanted, He could've made everyone on earth into believers, (but He didn't). So how can you make people believe when they don't want to? No soul can believe except by God's leave... (*Qur'an* 10:99-100)

> You can't impress them with a strong show of force, so instead remind with this Qur'an anyone who will fear My promise (of what is to come). (*Qur'an* 50:45)

> So obey God and obey His Messenger, though if anyone turns aside, Our Messenger's only duty is to convey (the message) clearly. (*Qur'an* 64:12)

> Say to them, "The truth (has now come to you) from your Lord." Whoever wants to believe (in it), will do so. Whoever wants to reject it, will do so. (*Qur'an* 18:29a)

ISLAM IS NOT AN ARAB RELIGION

An additional misconception is that Islam is an Arab religion. In point of fact, many Arabs are not Muslims. Iraq houses a Christian population of around one million Arabs. About 05% of the Arabs in Jordan are Christian, and higher percentages of Christians are to be found among the Arabs of Syria, Lebanon, and Palestine. Further, the vast majority of Muslims are not Arabs. There are over 160 million Muslims in Indonesia, over 100 million in Bangladesh, over 100 million in Nigeria, over 100 million in India, over 90 million in China, over 60 million in Turkey, and several million in Germany, France, and Great Britain.

With regard to Islam in America, it is currently estimated that there are over seven million Muslims in the United States, making it the second largest religion in the USA. Of those over seven million Muslims, it appears that somewhere between 30% and just over 50% are native-born Americans whose parents belong or had once belonged to some other religious tradition. In fact, American conversions to Islam range as high as 25,000 converts each year. During the last decade of the 20th century, the number of mosques in America has more than tripled, climbing from just over 600 to around 2,000. Currently, more Islamic books are being published in English than in Arabic.

CULTURE VS. ISLAM

As a final misconception, one must list the erroneous assumption that some of the worst cultural practices of so-called Muslim countries of the Third World are manifestations of Islam. Here, I am referring to such abominations as so-called "honor killings," the killing of civilian non-combatants, etc. These practices are no more representative of Islam than is the widespread practice of families in certain areas of so-called Catholic South America in selling their teenage daughters into white slavery a valid representation of Roman Catholicism. I urge you to differentiate between Islam and the cultural practices of certain Third-World areas. Likewise, I urge you to understand and appreciate that Osama bin Laden and Saddam Hussein are not representative of Islam.

CONCLUSIONS

As noted previously, misconceptions about Islam are prevalent throughout the Western world. The above list of misconceptions is hardly exhaustive. In fact, two of the most common misconceptions about Islam, i.e., that Jihad means "holy war" and that women are degraded and subjugated in Islam, were not even considered in the above list. Misconceptions about these two issues are so prevalent that each issue merits its own chapter at the end of this book.

Chapter Three
The Basics of Islam

PROPHET MUHAMMAD

BIRTH AND CHILDHOOD

Prophet Muhammad was born circa 570 CE in Makkah, the only child of 'Abdullah and Aminah. Prophet Muhammad's father died only weeks before Muhammad's birth, and Muhammad was initially raised by his mother. While still an infant, Muhammad was placed in the care of a wet nurse, Halimah bint Abu Du'ayb of the Bani Sa'd. The Bani Sa'd were Bedouins of the desert, and Muhammad spent his early years in the desert with Halimah's family. Sometime between the age of three and five, Muhammad was returned to his mother's care in Makkah.

When Muhammad was only six years old, his mother died during a trip to Madinah. Muhammad was then placed in the care of his paternal grandfather, 'Abd Al-Muttalib. While grandson and grandfather bonded closely, this bond was unfortunately quite short-lived, as 'Abd Al-Muttalib died when Muhammad was only eight years old. As a result, Muhammad was placed in the care of his paternal uncle, Abu Talib. Abu Talib was somewhat impoverished financially, and Muhammad spent most of the rest of his childhood working as a shepherd to help support the family.

As can be seen from the above, Prophet Muhammad's life consisted of a succession of major losses. His father died shortly before Muhammad was born. Beginning in infancy, he was separated from his mother for several years while he stayed with Halimah in the desert. Between the ages of three and five, he was returned to his mother, thus being separated from the only family he had known up until then. His mother then died when he was six, and his grandfather died when he was eight. Such devastating losses might have psychologically scarred another person. However, for Prophet Muhammad, they appear to have endowed him with a special sensitivity and kindness to orphans and the unfortunate.

When Muhammad was either nine or 12 years old, he accompanied his uncle, Abu Talib, on a caravan journey to Syria. En route, Muhammad met Bahira, a Christian monk, at Busra. The monk examined Muhammad and then pronounced that Muhammad was destined to be a prophet.

EARLY ADULTHOOD

By early adulthood, Muhammad had gained a sterling reputation for his honesty and trustworthiness. As such, he was called Al-Amin, i.e., the trustworthy. Because of his unblemished character, when he was about 24 years old, Muhammad was asked to lead a caravan to Syria for Khadijah, a wealthy widow who was Muhammad's senior by 15 years. En route, Nestor, another Christian monk, also announced that Muhammad was destined to be a prophet of God.

When Muhammad and the caravan returned to Makkah, Khadijah was overjoyed at the profit that she had made and by the reports she received about Muhammad's flawless character. She was also informed about Nestor's pronouncement and that at least one person in the caravan had briefly glimpsed two angels shading Muhammad from the desert sun. As such, even though she was wealthy and Muhammad was poor, and even though she was Muhammad's senior by 15 years, she sent an emissary proposing marriage. The proposal was accepted, and Muhammad married Khadijah when he was 25 years old. By all accounts the marriage was one of great happiness. Despite Khadijah's age, she bore six children to Muhammad—two sons dying during childhood and four daughters surviving into adulthood.

THE PROPHETIC CALL

Having married Khadijah, Muhammad was now able to devote himself to spiritual reflection and meditation. As such, he began to spend time in a cave on Mt. Hira, one of the mountains surrounding Makkah, where he could pursue his spiritual quest in privacy. On one of those retreats in his 40th year of life, i.e., in 610 CE, the angel Gabriel appeared to him and revealed the following words of God—the first verses of the Qur'an to be revealed to Prophet Muhammad.

Read in the name of your Lord Who created—created human beings from a clinging thing. Read, for your Lord is Most Generous. He taught with the pen; He taught human beings what they didn't know before. (Qur'an 96:1-5)

This initial experience with angel Gabriel terrified Prophet Muhammad. For a time, he feared that he was possessed by a jinn or losing his mind. In response, Khadijah consulted her cousin Waraqah, who was one of the very few Christians living among the pagans of Makkah. Waraqah listened to the story of Muhammad's encounter and quickly drew the conclusion that Muhammad had been visited by Gabriel and that Muhammad was destined to be a prophet who would be persecuted by his own people. Despite Waraqah's reassurance, Prophet Muhammad continued to have doubts about what had happened and about his own sanity. These doubts were subsequently relieved by a second revelation, the site and date of which are basically unknown.

> Nun. By the pen and what (scribes) record, by the grace of your Lord, you're not crazy. On the contrary, you're going to have an unfailing reward, for you have a most excellent character. (*Qur'an* 68:1-4)

After receiving this second revelation, the revelations stopped for a period of time that may have lasted anywhere from a few days to three years. However, once the revelations began again, they continued sporadically for the rest of Prophet Muhammad's life. As these revelations continued, Prophet Muhammad was instructed to begin proclaiming these revelations, privately at first to just his family and friends and later publicly to all that he met.

The public ministry of Prophet Muhammad began circa 613 CE and was met with scorn, ridicule, and resistance by most of the pagan polytheists of Makkah. Nonetheless, Muhammad continued his mission, proclaiming the Oneness of God and the revelations of the *Qur'an* to all who would listen. As his ministry began to gain momentum and converts, usually from the financially disadvantaged classes, the Makkans began to feel increasingly threatened by the monotheistic message being preached by Muhammad. As such, verbal and emotional persecution turned into physical abuse, and many early Muslims were mercilessly tortured.

In 617 CE, the persecution of Muhammad and the early Muslims reached its zenith. Muhammad, his family, and his entire tribal clan were quarantined in a hollow on the outskirts of Makkah. A complete social and economic boycott was conducted against them, and the Muslims were reduced to the covert purchase of contraband food at horribly inflated prices. After two years, the quarantine and boycott were finally lifted. However, the physical toll exacted by those two years no doubt contributed to the deaths of Khadijah and Abu Talib later in 619 CE.

While the quarantine and boycott had been lifted, the persecution otherwise continued. As such, in 622 CE, Prophet Muhammad followed other escaping Muslims to Madinah, a city north of Makkah that had offered to accept Prophet Muhammad and the Muslims of Makkah, had acknowledged that Muhammad was a prophet, and had agreed to follow and defend him. This migration from Makkah to Madinah in 622 CE is known as the *Hijrah*, and it marks the beginning of the Islamic lunar calendar.

THE PROPHET IN MADINAH

Having arrived in Madinah and being installed as the spiritual and temporal leader of Madinah, one of Prophet Muhammad's first acts was to issue the Covenant of Madinah, a document governing the two Arab tribes and three Jewish tribes of Madinah. The key provisions of the Covenant of Madinah are listed below.

THE COVENANT OF MADINAH

A.   PROVISIONS PERTAINING TO MUSLIMS AND ARABS

1. Those Muslims emigrating from Makkah to Madinah and the indigenous Arabs of Madinah form one *Ummah* (community) to the exclusion of all others.

2. Each tribe and clan is responsible for its own blood money, retribution fees, and ransom payments.

3. The believers shall not leave anyone destitute by refusing to pay blood money, retribution fees, or ransom payments.

4. All believers shall unite against anyone who is rebellious or seeks to spread enmity and sedition, regardless of family or tribal ties.

5. No believer may kill another believer or support an unbeliever against a believer.

6. The protection of God is extended to all believers, regardless of class or tribal background.

7. The believers are to support each other.

8. No believer may support a criminal or give him refuge.

B.   PROVISIONS PERTAINING TO THE JEWS OF MADINAH

1. The Jews are one community with the believers.

2. The Jews may continue to profess their own religion and are guaranteed the freedom of their own religious practices.

3. Any Jew who adheres to this covenant shall have the aide and succor of the believers and shall be entitled to all the rights pertaining to a believer.

4. Each tribe and clan of Jews is responsible for its own blood money, retribution fees, and ransom payments.

C. Provisions pertaining to both Jews and Arabs

1. The Jews and Arabs of Madinah enter into a mutual defense pact, with each group sustaining its own costs entailed by honoring this pact.

2. The Jews and Arabs of Madinah will hold counsel with each other, and mutual relations shall be founded on righteousness, while sin is prohibited.

3. Neither the Jews nor the Arabs shall commit sins to the prejudice of the other group.

4. If the Jews wrong the Arabs, or if the Arabs wrong the Jews, the wronged party shall be aided.

5. Madinah shall remain sacred and inviolate for all that join this covenant, except for those who perpetrate an injustice or crime.

6. All parties to this covenant are to boycott the non-Muslims of Makkah.

7. All parties to this covenant will defend Madinah from any foreign attack.

8. No provision of this covenant shall prohibit any party from seeking lawful retribution.

9. No party to this covenant may initiate war without the permission of the Prophet.

D. If a dispute arises between any two parties to this agreement, the dispute shall be submitted to God and His Messenger for arbitration.

With the issuance of the Covenant of Madinah and its ratification by both the Jews and Arabs of Madinah, an Islamic state was established for the first time. Prophet Muhammad now had to assume responsibility for guidance and governance in temporal and secular affairs. However, all was not settled. Among the Arabs of Madinah, numerous hypocrites covertly worked to bring down the Islamic state and to undermine Prophet Muhammad. While several Jews of Madinah converted to Islam and while others upheld the covenant of Madinah, e.g., Rabbi Mukhayriq who died at the Battle of Uhud while fighting alongside the Muslims against the Makkans, as a group, the three Jewish tribes of Madinah, one after another, allied with the pagans of Makkah and committed treason during times of war. As such, each tribe in turn was exiled from Madinah.

Despite Prophet Muhammad and most of the early Muslims having relocated to Madinah, the pagans of Makkah continued to harass and persecute the Muslims at every opportunity. On several occasions, the Makkans raised armies and attacked the Muslims of Madinah. Nonetheless, Prophet Muhammad continued to gain converts to Islam, and

Islam began to grow ever more rapidly throughout the Arabian Peninsula. As such, in 630 CE, Makkah fell to the Muslims without an attack even being necessary.

Following the conquest of and the cleansing of idol worship in Makkah, Prophet Muhammad returned to Madinah. During the subsequent months, the fold of Islam grew ever more rapidly, as more and more people accepted Islam. Prophet Muhammad and Islam were now a force to be reckoned with across most of the Arabian Peninsula. Nonetheless, the Prophet continued his humble lifestyle. In many ways, he was a king in all but title, but he continued to live no differently than the humblest of the subjects of the realm. Whatever wealth came to him was quickly distributed to the poor and needy. He could have been king, but he was far more—he was the prophet and messenger of God.

Beginning on the eighth of the lunar month of Dhul-Hijjah of the 10th *Hijri* year (Saturday, March 10, 632 CE), having previously traveled from Madinah to Makkah, the Prophet began the performance of Hajj during his Farewell Pilgrimage. His manner and practice in performing this Hajj set standard and example for all subsequent Hajj pilgrimages to Makkah. Even today, around three million Muslims every year faithfully follow the example of the Prophet's Farewell Pilgrimage.

Returning to Madinah following the Farewell Pilgrimage, the Prophet's health grew steadily weaker. Finally, on the 12th of the lunar month of Rabi' Al-Awwal in the 11th *Hijri* year (Monday, June 11, 632 CE), Prophet Muhammad died.

THE *QUR'AN* AND *SUNNAH*

INTRODUCTION

With the death of Prophet Muhammad in 632 CE, Muslims lost both their spiritual guide and temporal ruler. No longer was the Prophet there to instruct them with his teaching and with his behavioral example of conduct and religious practice. No longer was there a person to whom to turn for completely authoritative answers to spiritual doubts and religious questions. However, all was not lost. Prophet Muhammad had bequeathed two crucial legacies that would serve Muslims in the following centuries. The first was the *Qur'an*, and the second was his *Sunnah* (customary religious practice).

THE *QUR'AN*

As noted previously, Prophet Muhammad received the first portion of the *Qur'an* in 610 CE. Angel Gabriel visited the Prophet while he was engaged in a spiritual retreat in a cave on Mt. Hira and delivered to him the dictated words of God. Over the course of the next 22 years, Gabriel brought revelation after revelation in an episodic manner, with each such revelation finding its place in the *Qur'an*. As these revelations were delivered to the Prophet, he would memorize them and recite them to others who also memorized them. In addition, each such revelation was written down by the Prophet's scribes and other literate Muslims on whatever material was present, including stones, palm leaves, animal skins, bones, what paper was available, etc.

One year after the Prophet's death, Abu Bakr, the first caliph, i.e., successor to the Prophet, ordered that the complete set of revelations be collected and written down in a single book. During the rule of 'Uthman ibn 'Affan, the third caliph, four copies of the *Qur'an* were made utilizing the copy that was constructed under Abu Bakr, at least one of which survives to this day. Of note, there have been no additions or deletions to the *Qur'an* since the first recension of Abu Bakr.

For Muslims, there can be no higher religious authority than the *Qur'an*. The *Qur'an* is seen as standing uniquely alone as the only book of revelation preserved in its original and pristine purity. For over 1.6 billion Muslims the world over, the *Qur'an* is the immaculate recording of the verbatim words of God as revealed by Gabriel to Prophet Muhammad. These are not the words of Prophet Muhammad as inspired by God, but the actual words of revelation sent by God to Prophet Muhammad.

THE *SUNNAH*

The *Sunnah* refers to the religious teaching and customary religious practice of Prophet Muhammad. With regard to the *Sunnah*, the *Qur'an* repeatedly proclaims that Muslims are to obey Prophet Muhammad and to follow his illustrious example of behavior and conduct. As such, the *Sunnah* of Prophet Muhammad is religiously authoritative and binding on all Muslims.

Given that Muslims are to follow the *Sunnah* of Prophet Muhammad, how are Muslims to know what was the actual *Sunnah* of Prophet Muhammad? The answers are to be found in the *Ahadith* (singular = *Hadith*), which are narratives concerning what Prophet Muhammad reportedly said and did. However, let us be clear that it is the actual *Sunnah* of Prophet Muhammad that is religiously authoritative upon Muslims, not the *Ahadith* per se. Not all *Ahadith* were created equal. Some appear to have a stronger provenance than others, and some *Ahadith* were clearly fabricated, a fact that leads to the all-important topic of the provenance and authenticity of any given *Hadith*.

Over the first three centuries following the death of Prophet Muhammad, many *Ahadith* scholars categorized the various *Ahadith* and compiled those considered to be accurate and genuine into major collections. Over time, six of these collections came to be almost universally regarded within Sunni Islam as being religiously authoritative. These are referred to as the *Al-Kutub Al-Sittah*, i.e., the six books. These six collections may be considered to be the six "standard" collections of *Ahadith* and consist of the collections of Al-Bukhari, Muslim, Abu Dawud, Al-Tirmidhi, Al-Nasa'i, and Ibn Majah.

SUMMARY

The *Qur'an* and *Sunnah* are the foundations of Islam. The former consists of God's actual words as given to Prophet Muhammad through Gabriel. As such, the *Qur'an* is the highest religious authority available to Muslims. In contrast, the *Sunnah* consists of Prophet Muhammad's teaching and typical pattern of conduct regarding religious matters. The *Sunnah* was preserved within the *Ahadith*, and elaborate and demanding criteria were developed by early Muslim scholars in order to: authenticate the provenance of individual *Hadith*, and verify whether or not a given *Hadith* accurately preserved the *Sunnah* of Prophet Muhammad. As such, the *Sunnah* is second only to the *Qur'an* as a source of religious authority and guidance in Islam.

FIVE ARTICLES OF FAITH

The *Qur'an* specifically mentions five primary articles of faith that Muslims must accept and believe. (1) Muslims believe that there is no god but the One God and that only God is worthy of worship. This essential Oneness of God precludes His having any associates or partners. (2) Muslims believe in all the messengers and prophets of God without differentiating hierarchically among them and without elevating them beyond their human nature. (3) Muslims believe in all the scriptures and revelations from God as they were delivered in their original form. However, only the last book from God, i.e., the *Qur'an*, continues to exist on Earth in its original and pristine form. (4) Muslims believe in the angels of God but realize that they are no more than one of God's creations. (5) Muslims believe in life after death, an ultimate Day of Judgment, and a Hereafter containing both Heaven and Hell.

THE PILLARS OF PRACTICE

Within Islam, there are five fundamental pillars of religious practice and worship. These include: (1) the *Shahadah* or testimonial of faith, which consists of understanding and testifying to the fact that there is no god besides the One God and that Muhammad was the Messenger of God; (2) performing the *Salat* or five daily, obligatory prayers of worship within their appointed times; (3) the payment of *Zakat* or obligatory charity to those in need, which in most non-agricultural contexts refers to 02.5% of the economic surplus that one has held for one full year; (4) *Sawm* or fasting from dawn to sunset during the lunar month of Ramadan, a practice that is conditional upon the physical and medical wellbeing of the individual; and (5) Hajj or performing the pilgrimage to Makkah during the lunar month of Dhul-Hijjah at least once during a person's lifetime, a practice that is conditional upon the individual having the physical and financial resources to make this trip.

Chapter Four

DIFFERENCES BETWEEN ISLAM AND CHRISTIANITY

INTRODUCTION

Towards the close of chapter 1, several differences were listed among the Abrahamic faiths. In this chapter, four of those differences that divide Christianity and Islam are examined. However, before beginning this endeavor, it should be noted that early Christianity was not a single, monolithic structure. There were many branches to early Christianity, and each local church, e.g., the church at Corinth and the church at Jerusalem, was independent of every other church. Each church had its own ecclesiastical hierarchy, its own set of recognized scripture, and its own doctrine and dogma. Such differences were especially apparent when one considers the four issues under consideration in this chapter. As will be shown, there were branches of early Christianity that approached each of the four issues under consideration in a manner quite consistent with Islamic interpretation and at variance with contemporary Christianity.

THE MISSION AND MINISTRY OF JESUS

Qur'an 3:49 informs the reader that Jesus was appointed by God as a messenger to the Children of Israel. In contrast, contemporary Christianity typically maintains that Jesus' ministry and mission were to the world at large. Nonetheless, there are several New Testament passages that appear to agree with the Islamic position that he was sent only to the Children of Israel. For example, consider the following Biblical verses.

These twelve Jesus sent out with the following instructions: "Go nowhere among the Gentiles, and enter no town of the Samaritans, but go rather to the lost sheep of the house of Israel." (Matthew 10:5-6).

Jesus left that place and went away to the district of Tyre and Sidon. Just then a Canaanite woman from that region came out and started shouting, "Have mercy on me, Lord, Son of David, my daughter is tormented by a demon." But he did not answer her at all. And his disciples came and urged him, saying, "Send her away, for she keeps shouting after us." He answered, "I was sent only to the lost sheep of the house of Israel." But she came and knelt before him, saying,

"Lord, help me." He answered, "It is not fair to take the children's food and throw it to the dogs." She said, "Yes, Lord, yet even the dogs eat the crumbs that fall from their masters' table." Then Jesus answered her, "Woman, great is your faith! Let it be done for you as you wish." And her daughter was healed instantly. (Matthew 15:21-28)

We might also consider how the actual disciples of Jesus, as well as the immediate followers of those disciples, continued Jesus' ministry after the end of his earthly sojourn. However, at this point we must interject a very important proviso that is often overlooked by contemporary Christians, namely that Paul (a former Pharisee and rabbi once known as Saul of Tarsus) was never a disciple of Jesus and apparently never even met Jesus during the latter's earthly ministry. In short, Paul, who was the foremost proponent of the concept of a universal ministry for Jesus, does not represent the tradition of the disciples of Jesus and, in fact, was frequently in marked conflict with the Jerusalem church, which was the headquarters of the actual disciples of Jesus. This can be readily substantiated by turning to the following New Testament passages: Galatians 2:1-9 and Acts 9:26; 15:1-5; and 21:17-26. So how did the actual disciples and their followers continue Jesus' ministry? The answer may be found in the following verse.

Now those who were scattered because of the persecution that took place over Stephen traveled as far as Phoenicia, Cyprus, and Antioch, and they spoke the word to no one except Jews. (Acts 11:19)

Many scholars of the history of early Christianity, recognizing that the actual disciples of Jesus did not preach to other than the Children of Israel, refer to the Jerusalem church as being Jewish-Christian. This Jewish-Christian tradition continued long after the destruction of the Temple of Jerusalem in 70 CE. Such early Christian movements as the Ebionites, the Nazarenes, and the Elkasites represented this Jewish-Christian tradition. In particular, we can point to the Ebionites, who fled to Jordan, Syria, Turkey, and Egypt following the destruction of the Temple in 70 CE. Of note, the Ebionites continued as a viable movement within greater Christianity through the second, third, and fourth centuries CE. Likewise, the Nazarenes were known to have existed in greater Syria at least as late as the fourth century CE.

Reviewing the preceding historical record, one finds evidence of a trajectory within early Christianity that can be traced back to Matthew, Acts, and the Jerusalem church, that continued to exist well into at least the fourth century CE, and that continued to restrict active preaching to the "Children of Israel."

THE CRUCIFIXION

Any student of comparative religion knows that there are major similarities in the understanding of Jesus and Mary by Islam and early Christianity. However, when it comes to the crucifixion event, we find a fundamental discrepancy between Islam and modern Christianity. The *Qur'an* declares that Jesus was not crucified, even though his persecutors thought that they had crucified him, a position in marked conflict with contemporary Christianity. Instead, God saved Jesus and "raised (Jesus) up to Himself," a statement having parallels with the ascension of Jesus as portrayed in Mark 16:19 and Luke 24:50-51.

> ...they suppressed (God's truth), made unfounded accusations against Mary, and boasted, "We killed Jesus, the Messiah, the son of Mary." However, they didn't kill him, nor did they crucify him, but it was made to appear to them that they did. Those who argue about it are full of doubts and have no (concrete) information. On the contrary, they only follow theories, for they certainly didn't kill him. Certainly not! God raised (Jesus) up to Himself, for God is powerful and wise. (*Qur'an* 4:156-158)

For most modern Christians, indeed, for most inhabitants of the Western world, it is almost unthinkable that anyone could seriously maintain that Jesus was not crucified. Critics of Islam might even maintain that the alleged resurrection of Jesus is a matter of religious belief but that the crucifixion of Jesus is a matter of an unblemished historical record. However, the actual historical record is otherwise than one might expect.

Outside of the New Testament and other early Christian writings, there are only two references to Jesus being crucified in the entire historical record of the first and early second centuries. The first was made by Josephus, a first-century Jewish historian, and the second by Tacitus, a first and second-century Roman. Neither writer was a witness to the crucifixion event. For that matter, most Biblical scholars maintain that none of the New Testament authors who wrote about the crucifixion were actual witnesses to that event. Nonetheless, the skeptic of the Islamic position that Jesus was not crucified will insist that any serious attempt to refute the crucifixion of Jesus must marshal an impressive array of documentation that there was serious controversy about whether or not Jesus was actually crucified. "Where is that documentation?" they may well ask.

The answer is that it is to be found within the writings of early Christianity itself. For example, the writings of the Apostolic Fathers frequently noted that there were Christian sects that rejected the proposition that Jesus had been crucified. Such references can be found in the writings of Ignatius, Polycarp, Justin, Irenaeus, Tertullian, and Hippolytus. Together, these Apostolic Fathers represent a veritable "who's who" of early Christianity. As a specific example, we can turn to the *Trallians*, a book authored by Bishop Ignatius of Antioch, who died circa 110 CE. In referring to the crucifixion event, Ignatius wrote that there were Christians of his day who denied that Jesus was crucified in reality and maintained that he was crucified only in appearance or in illusion.

> But if, as some say...his suffering was only an appearance, then why am I a prisoner, and why do I long to fight with the wild beasts? In that case, I am dying in vain.

In considering the above quotation, one must acknowledge that Ignatius could not be attacking a belief among early Christians that did not already exist. His attack against those Christians who believed that Jesus' crucifixion was only illusory demonstrates the existence of that belief among Christians as early as 110 CE, i.e., by the time of Ignatius' death. Further, the fact that Ignatius even bothered to attack this doctrine suggests that the belief in the illusory nature of the crucifixion was quite widespread by 110 CE.

That many branches of early Christianity maintained that it was not Jesus who was crucified can also be verified by considering the New Testament Apocrypha. For example, the Apocalypse of Peter 81:4-82:33 maintained that Jesus was crucified only in appearance, not in reality, with the one who was crucified being a substitute or simulacrum of Jesus. Likewise, the Second Treatise of the Great Seth 55:10-56:25 stated that it was not Jesus who was crucified, but Simon (presumably Simon of Cyrene, who is identified in Matthew 27:32, Mark 15:21, and Luke 23:26 as being the person who carried Christ's cross for him). Seth goes on to state that Simon appeared as though he were Jesus. This position, i.e., that it was Simon of Cyrene who was crucified in place of Jesus, was a cardinal tenet of the early Christian group known as Basilideans, which flourished in Egypt during the second century CE. Of note, the Basilideans claimed that they received their information from Glaucus, whom they claimed was the translator for Simon Peter, the disciple of Jesus. Finally, the Acts of John 97-101 reported that the crucifixion of Jesus was an illusion.

However, it is not just within the apocryphal writings that one finds evidence that it was not Jesus who was crucified. The Biblical book of Matthew 27:11-26 states that Pontius Pilate, the Roman governor of Judea, gave the crowd a choice between releasing "Jesus who is called the Messiah" or "Jesus Barabbas." (For any Christians who might wonder about the name "Jesus Barabbas," I would refer you to the New Revised Standard Version of Matthew 27:17 for this identification, which is based on some of the oldest surviving texts of this verse.) Matthew then goes on to state that the crowd chose Jesus Barabbas and that Pilate released Jesus Barabbas. Of note, "Barabbas" may be translated from the Aramaic as "son of the father." In short, Matthew tells us that Pilate released "Jesus, the son of the Father," and condemned a different Jesus, who was claiming to be the messiah. So, who was who? Certainly, Matthew raises the very real question of who was actually released and who was actually crucified.

However, if Jesus was not crucified, what does this say about the Christian doctrine of the atonement in the blood, i.e., forgiveness of sin based upon Christ's crucifixion? After all, was not the crucifixion of Jesus the crowning pinnacle of his divine mission? Was it not an absolutely indispensable part of his divine work? Jesus' own answer to these questions appears to be reported in a prayer attributed to Jesus in the Gospel of John. Of note, John places this prayer prior to the crucifixion event.

And this is eternal life, that they may know you, the only true God, and Jesus Christ whom you have sent. I glorified you on earth by finishing the work that you gave me to do. (John 17:3-4)

"I...finish(ed) the work that you gave me to do" and did so prior to the crucifixion event. As reported by John, Jesus specifically excluded the later crucifixion event as being part of his "work that you gave me to do."

THE NATURE OF JESUS

Islam holds that Jesus was a man, but one who was selected by God to be a prophet and messenger. Despite Islam's adherence to the virgin birth of Jesus, Islam maintains that Jesus was created by God, not begotten by Him.

Say (to them): "He is only one God—God the Eternal Absolute. He neither begets nor was He begotten, and there is nothing equal to Him. (Qur'an 112:1-4)

"But my Lord!" she (Mary) cried out. "How can I have a son when no man has touched me?" "And so it is that God creates whatever He wants," the angels replied. "When He decides something, He only has to say, 'Be,' and it is."... The example of Jesus in the sight of God is like that of Adam. He created him from dust, saying, "Be," and he was. (Qur'an 3:47, 59)

(Jesus) was no more than a servant to whom We granted Our favor. We made him an example for the Children of Israel. (*Qur'an* 43:59)

When considering the issue of the nature of Jesus within early Christianity, one is immediately confronted with the major differences that existed among various early Christian churches. At the risk of oversimplifying, the ways in which early Christianity answered the question of the nature of Jesus can be grouped into three broad categories: Jesus was God, Jesus was man and God simultaneously, and Jesus was a man.

The first position, i.e., that Jesus was God, denies the humanity of Jesus. This position was represented in early Christianity by many forms of Christian Gnosticism, especially by Docetism. The Docetist position was that Jesus did not have a real or material body, but only a phantom or apparent body. As such, the Docetists maintained that Jesus could not have died on the cross because he did not have a physical body. Likewise, because he had no physical body, there could have been no resurrection.

The second position, i.e., that Jesus was both God and man simultaneously, is the one that evolved into the typical and orthodox doctrines of contemporary Christianity. That Jesus is neither simply God, nor simply man, but is both God and man simultaneously is directly stated in the so-called Nicene Creed issued by the Council of Constantinople in 381 CE and in the creedal formulation issued by the Council of Ephesus in 431 CE. However, the simultaneous god-man dichotomy finds its fullest expression in the statement issued by the Council of Chalcedon in 451 CE:

> ...our Lord Jesus Christ, perfect in deity and perfect in humanity...in two natures, without being mixed, transmuted, divided, or separated. The distinction between the natures is by no means done away with through the union, but rather the identity of each nature is preserved and concurs into one person and being.

There are two natures that are neither "mixed" nor "separated." If they are neither "mixed" nor "separated," then what are they? Clearly, this is a doctrine that can be promulgated only through recourse to the phrase "divine mystery," because the doctrine that there is something that is neither "mixed" nor "separated" defies all human logic.

The third position, i.e., that Jesus was a man, although one standing in a special relationship with God, is represented in early Christianity by the various Adoptionist theologies, including Dynamic Monarchianism, Arianism, Nestorianism, the Paulicians of Armenia, etc. These early Christian movements basically maintained that Jesus' relationship to God was like that of an adopted son to his adoptive father, not like a begotten son to his begetting father. This position is more or less consistent with Islamic thought, which views Jesus as being a man, albeit as a man who was a prophet and messenger of God, and who thus stood in a special relationship with God.

The Adoptionist trajectory in early Christianity begins with the baptism of Jesus by John the Baptist. According to most Adoptionists, it was at this moment that Jesus moved into his special relationship with God, not at his conception or birth. With regard to the baptism, the account of the Gospel of Luke is especially relevant. As noted in appropriate footnotes to the New Revised Standard Version of the *Bible*, the oldest Greek manuscripts of and quotations from Luke render the key verse in question as follows.

> Now when all the people were baptized, and when Jesus also had been baptized and was praying, the heaven was opened, and the Holy Spirit descended upon him in bodily form like a dove. And a voice came from heaven, "You are my son; today I have begotten you." (Luke 3:21-22)

"Today I have begotten you," i.e., at the time of baptism, not at the time of conception. Given that Jesus was clearly an adult at the time of his baptism, under this ancient reading of Luke, "begotten" must be understood metaphorically, not physically or literally. In other words, the "sonship" of Jesus was a created relationship, not a begotten relationship. Furthermore, before the contemporary Christian rejects this probably original wording of Luke 3:22, he or she should consider that this exact wording is also found in Hebrews 1:5a, Hebrews 5:5, and Acts 13:33, in what are obvious references to the baptism of Jesus. This same wording is also to be found in Psalms 2:7 and in the Gospel of the Ebionites, the latter of which reads as follows.

> When the people were baptized, Jesus also came and was baptized by John...And a voice (sounded) from heaven that said: "You are my beloved son; in you I am well pleased." And again: "I have this day begotten you." (Gospel of the Ebionites, as quoted by Epiphanius in *Panarian* 30.13.7-8)

Given this scriptural legacy, it is not surprising that Adoptionism was a potent force within early Christianity from the first through the seventh centuries. In fact, one can trace the chronological trajectory of Adoptionism and related subordinationist Christologies with some precision.

As early as the first century CE, the Adoptionist position was a key doctrine of the Ebionites, who maintained that Jesus became the messiah and adopted son of God at his baptism and that this was secondary to Jesus having obeyed the Mosaic Law. Circa 100 CE, Elkasai, the founder of the Elkasites, began to preach an early Christian doctrine in Parthia. Central to the preaching of Elkasai was the concept that Jesus Christ was simply a prophet of God.

Circa 189 CE, Theodotus the Tanner traveled from Byzantium to Rome, where he propounded an Adoptionist position that maintained that Jesus was a mere man, although miraculously conceived. According to Theodotus, Jesus was the metaphorical son of God only to the extent that God granted him divine wisdom and power at his baptism. Despite being excommunicated by Pope Victor I, Theodotus acquired numerous followers who continued his Adoptionist preaching, which began to be known as Theodotianism or Dynamic Monarchianism. This movement lasted well into the third century CE.

Origen (circa 185-254 CE) was a celebrated writer, theologian, and priest who contributed numerous volumes to early Christian literature. Among the notable aspects of Origen's theology was his insistence that "the Son (was) inferior to the Father." Clearly a subordinationist when it came to the nature of Jesus, Origen's teachings were later to influence Dionysius of Alexandria, Eusebius of Nicomedia, Arius, and the rise of Arianism.

Dionysius of Alexandria became head of the catechetical school at Alexandria circa 231 CE and Bishop of Alexandria in 248 CE, thus becoming one of the five princes or patriarchs of the church, a position that he held until 264 CE. Following in the footsteps of Origen, Dionysius stressed the subordination of Jesus to God, arguing that Jesus did not exist before being engendered, that therefore there was a time in which Jesus did not exist, and that therefore Jesus was not eternal. Not being eternal, Jesus had to be a creation and product that was foreign to the being and substance of God, just as the vine is foreign to the gardener and the ship is foreign to the ship builder. As will be seen, Dionysius was hardly the last bishop, patriarch, and prince of the church to take this position.

Circa 260 CE, Paul of Samosata, Bishop and Patriarch of Antioch, also advanced the Adoptionist position. Paul held that Jesus was a man who was born of Mary and that Jesus was divine only to the extent that he was the human vehicle through whom God spoke. Paul's Adoptionist message was picked up by his followers, who later evolved into the Paulicians of Armenia, a Christian movement active as late as the seventh century CE.

St. Lucian of Antioch (circa 240-312 CE) was a celebrated Christian teacher and theologian, whose theological formulations regarding the nature of Jesus appeared to have been influenced by Paul of Samosata. Despite his Adoptionist teachings regarding the nature of Jesus, Lucian was canonized a saint of the church, in part secondary to his being tortured and starved to death for his refusal to eat meat that had been ritually offered to the pagan gods of Rome during the persecution of Christians by Emperor Maximinus.

The Adoptionist position in early Christianity reached its zenith under the teachings of Arius (circa 250-335 CE), a priest in Alexandria, Egypt. Arius taught that God is absolutely unique and incomparable, is alone self-existent, unchangeable, and infinite, and must be understood in terms of his absolute Oneness. Given this all-important first premise, Arius concluded that: (1) the life of Jesus as portrayed in the Biblical gospels demonstrates that Jesus was not self-existent, that he changed and grew over time, if in no other way than in passing through the stages of birth, childhood, adolescence, and adulthood, and that he was finite, having a definite time of conception and birth. Therefore, (2) Jesus was God's created being, who was called into existence out of nothingness, who could not have shared in the absolute uniqueness, immutability, and infinity of the Godhead without compromising them, who could not have been of the same substance as God without compromising the Oneness of God, and who could have had no direct knowledge of God, other than that which God chose to reveal to him.

It was due to the rapid rise of Arianism that the Synod at Alexandria met in September of 323 CE and formally excommunicated Arius. However, this excommunication was promptly reversed at the Synod of Bithynia in October of 323 CE. Finally, Emperor Constantine was forced to convene the Council of Nicaea in May of 325 CE, which formalized the doctrine that Jesus was of one substance with the Father. Arius refused to sign this creed and was thence branded as a heretic. However, the Arian position within Christianity was so strong that Constantine was forced to reinstate Arius at the Synod of Jerusalem in 335 CE. Later that same year, Arius died at Constantinople.

However, that was hardly the end of Arianism within early Christianity. Quite simply, despite the verdict of the Council of Nicaea, Arianism was probably the dominant Christology within fourth-century Christianity. In fact, in response to the continued growth of Arianism, the Council of Antioch in 341 CE released a new creed that omitted any mention of Jesus and God being of one substance. Apparently, the bishops gathered at the Council of Antioch, while rejecting the earlier findings of the Council of Nicaea, were unable to agree on any formulation regarding the relationship of Jesus to God.

In the middle of the fourth century CE, a modified form of Arianism (semi-Arianism) was propounded by Macedonius, the Bishop and Patriarch of Constantinople (339-341 and 351-360 CE), arguably a position secondary only to the Pope in the hierarchy of the church. While the formal teachings of Macedonius regarding the nature of Jesus appear to have oscillated somewhat over time, there is little doubt that he did what he could to repress the formulation derived at Nicaea that Jesus and God were of one substance.

Circa 350 CE, Aetius, a priest at Antioch, taught that God had always existed and that self-existence is part of the very essence of God, while Jesus was created by God. Given these premises, Aetius argued that Jesus was not consubstantial with God and was totally different than God, giving rise to the Anomoeist movement in fourth-century Christianity. While excommunicated for his Arianism, Aetius was reinstated by Eudoxius, Bishop of Antioch, and was made a bishop by Emperor Julian in 361.

The teachings of Aetius garnered tremendous support within Syria and the Middle East, in part due to his irrefutable logic as expressed in 300 syllogisms, all but 47 of which were later lost to recorded history. Furthermore, his position was ratified and endorsed by the Council of Sirmium in 357 CE. This council issued a creedal formulation that said that Jesus was "unlike" (*anomoios*) God. In short, based upon the position taken at the Council of Sirmium, the "official" position of Christianity in 357 CE was that Jesus Christ was "unlike" God and was of a different substance than God!

Only in 381 CE, at the Council of Constantinople, attended by only about 150 bishops, none of whom represented Western Christianity, was the Arian position finally laid to rest by the ecclesiastical structure of the church with the issuance of the so-called Nicene Creed. Notwithstanding this ecclesiastical dismissal, Arianism continued to flourish in many Christian areas and was a potent force within some Germanic tribes until the end of the seventh century. Even today, Arianism continues to be influential in the Unitarian movement and among the Jehovah Witnesses, who regard Arius as a forerunner of their founder, Charles Taze Russell.

In summary, early Christianity was quite conflicted about the issue of the nature of Jesus. The various Adoptionist positions within early Christianity were numerous and at times dominant. One can even speculate that Arian Christianity might well be a very sizable force within Christianity today if it were not for the fact that this branch of Christianity was so similar to the Islamic teaching regarding the nature of Jesus that it quite naturally was absorbed into Islam beginning in the seventh century CE.

THE NATURE OF GOD

Islam and modern Christianity differ concerning the nature of God, although several branches of early Christianity were in basic agreement with the Islamic concept of a strict and uncompromising monotheism, with God being seen as One and Indivisible.

Followers of Earlier Revelation! Don't go to extremes in your religious (doctrines), and don't make statements about God that aren't true. Jesus, the son of Mary, was a messenger from God and His (creative) word bestowed upon (the virgin) Mary and a spirit sent from Him. So believe in God and His messengers (who were mortal men). Don't say, "Trinity." Don't do it, as that would be best for you. Truly, God is just one God, glory be to Him! He's (far above) having a child! He owns everything in the heavens and on the earth, and God is quite enough to take care of matters (for Himself)! (*Qur'an* 4:171)

Now they're claiming, "God has begotten a son!" Glory be to Him! He's the Self-Sufficient! Everything in the heavens and on the earth belongs to Him! You have no basis to make such a claim! Are you saying things about God about which you know nothing? (*Qur'an* 10:68)

He hasn't taken any son, nor does He have any partners in His dominion. He created everything and measured their proportion exactly. (*Qur'an* 25:2)

Say (to them): "He is only one God—God the Eternal Absolute. He neither begets nor was He begotten, and there is nothing equal to Him." (*Qur'an* 112:1-4)

In contrast, when we examine the Christian concept of a Trinity, we find something that is totally foreign to both Judaism and Islam. There is no Islamic or Judaic equivalent to the notion of three persons in one substance. With regard to Judaism, the *Shema* of the Old Testament is quite clear in rejecting any concept of the deity other than the Unity and Oneness of God.

Hear, O Israel, the Lord our God, the Lord is One. (Deuteronomy 6:4)

A pronounced emphasis on the Unity of God is not limited to the Old Testament portion of the *Bible*. Not only does the word "Trinity" never occur in the *Bible*, the New Testament reports that Jesus also stressed the Unity and Oneness of God.

One of the scribes came near and heard them disputing with one another, and seeing that he answered them well, he asked him, "Which commandment is the first of all?" Jesus answered, "The first is, 'Hear, O Israel: the Lord our God, the Lord is one...'" (Mark 12:28-29)

Given the above considerations, it is not surprising that the early Apostolic Fathers were typically unwilling or not interested in speculating about the relationship of the Father, Son, and Holy Spirit. Other than directly supporting the divinity of the Son and/or indirectly maintaining the divinity of the Holy Spirit, such early Christian luminaries as Ignatius, Justin Martyr, and Irenaeus were unwilling to proceed in developing any conceptualization of a Trinity. Later theologians were more willing to speculate, with such speculation resulting in the Christian concept of the Trinity.

In contrast to the Christian concept of the "Son of God," Islam views Jesus as a resolute prophet of God. In contrast to the Christian concept of the Holy Spirit as the third person of one substance comprising the Trinity, Islam sees the Holy Spirit as being a title belonging to the angel Gabriel.

However, it is not just Islam and Judaism that reject the traditional Christian formulation of the Trinity. The early Christian churches were quite divided with regard to the conceptualized nature of God. To a great extent, these intra-Christian differences were directly related to the intra-Christian differences that existed concerning the nature of Jesus. Thus, the Jesus-as-man proponents within early Christianity, e.g., the Ebionites, Elkasites, Dynamic Monarchianism, Arianism, and Anomoeism denied the concept of a Trinitarian God and professed the Unity of God and the humanity of a created and finite Jesus. With regard to this issue, these branches of early Christianity were once again basically consistent with Islamic belief, which holds to a strict monotheism in proclaiming the Oneness and Unity of God.

However, it was not just the adoptionists within early Christianity who rejected the Trinitarian concept. Early Christianity was also characterized by groups known as subordinationists, who insisted that Jesus Christ was subordinate to God. While all Adoptionists were subordinationists, one could be a subordinationist without being an Adoptionist. Thus, Origen of Alexandria (185-254 CE) is sometimes called the father of Arianism, because he held that Jesus was subordinate to the Father and that the Holy Spirit was subordinate to both the Father and the Son.

Yet another subordinationist group within early Christianity, variously known as Macedonians and Pneumatomachians, believed that the Holy Spirit was essentially inferior to both the Father and the Son. Under the leadership of Macedonius, this group held a middle position between the Arians and those who proclaimed the divinity of Jesus, but were firmly anti-Trinitarian when it came to the Holy Spirit.

As should be clear by now, the doctrine of the Trinity developed gradually over several centuries, and not without substantial controversy and rejection. Throughout its first several centuries, Christianity struggled to maintain a strict monotheistic outlook, while still paying homage to the Father, Jesus, and the Holy Spirit. One solution, represented primarily by the various Adoptionists, was to subordinate Jesus to God. It was only with the Council of Nicaea in 325 CE that the doctrine that Jesus was of one substance with the Father began to be formulated in any real sense, although even at Nicaea, precious little was said about the Holy Spirit. Further, as previously noted, there was little unity at Nicaea, and what there was occurred only under the force of arms provided by Constantine. However, by the end of the fourth century CE, the Trinitarian concept of Christianity was on its way to being established as "official" doctrine.

God willing, the above review has illustrated that the early Christian churches were in fundamental disagreement when it came to the issue of the nature of God. Those who stressed the Unity of God via one or another of the subordinationist or Adoptionist positions were generally consistent with the Islamic position of the Oneness and Unity of God.

SUMMARY AND CONCLUSIONS

In conclusion, the historical record is clear. Throughout the first several centuries of Christianity, one can trace an Islamic or near-Islamic trajectory through all four issues under consideration.

Chapter Five

JIHAD-A DISTORTED
AND MISUNDERSTOOD CONCEPT

INTRODUCTION

Contrary to popular opinion, the Arabic word "Jihad" does not mean "holy war." The noun "Jihad" is from the Arabic verb "*Jahada,*" which means "to strive or to exert." Thus, the correct translation of Jihad is striving, exertion, or effort. Within an Islamic context, Jihad means striving for the sake of God. Thus, any activity in which one strives for the sake of God is Jihad. Further, of the 36 times that the word "Jihad" and its derivatives occur in the *Qur'an*, not one instance refers to actual war. In fact, the most prevalent form of Jihad is preaching and religious and moral exhortation.

Jihad as exhortation may take many forms. The verbal invitation to non-Muslims to enter into the fold of Islam is Jihad. Offering polite, verbal disapproval of the traditional worship of non-Muslims is Jihad. Verbal firmness in presenting the truth, especially as it relates to issues of religion, morality, and justice, is Jihad. Educating others about the *Qur'an* is Jihad, as is illustrated in the following passage from the *Qur'an*.

> So don't pay attention to those who suppress (their faith), but rather strive [Jihad] against them using (the logic) of this (Qur'an) with your utmost capacity. (*Qur'an* 25:52)

How does one strive against someone with the *Qur'an*? The Qur'an consists of God's revelation, and one strives against others with the *Qur'an* through the medium of preaching and verbal exhortation, whether in oral or written form. This conclusion is echoed in the following *Hadith*, in which Prophet Muhammad emphasized the superiority of Jihad as exhortation.

> The Messenger of God said, "The best fighting (Jihad) in the path of God is (to speak) a word of justice to an oppressive ruler." (*Abu Dawud, Hadith* #4330)

What should be the nature of that "word of justice to an oppressive ruler?" The instructions given to Prophet Moses serve as an example to all Muslims. One is to speak mildly and not belligerently.

Go to Pharaoh, for he's (a tyrant who's) gone out of control. Speak mildly to him, however, for he might heed the reminder or fear (God). (Qur'an 20:43-44)

In summary, Jihad means effort, striving, or exertion, and the highest form of Jihad is Jihad as exhortation. Jihad may also refer to an individual's struggle against his own base instincts or to any other effort engaged in for the sake of God, including marriage, parenting, being a good neighbor, etc. A man engages in Jihad when, for the sake of God, he strives to be a good husband to his wife and a good father to his children. A person practices Jihad when, for the sake of God, he attempts to benefit his neighbor and his fellow man. A person even practices Jihad when, for the sake of God, he expends the effort to smile at others.

Ibn Rushed (Averroes) wrote in his *Muqaddimaat* that there were at least four primary types of Jihad: by the heart, by the tongue, by the hand, and by the sword. Jihad by the heart refers to struggling to make faith a spiritual force in one's own life. Jihad by the tongue is preaching the universal truth of Islam and exhorting oneself and one's listeners to live a life of righteous conduct. Jihad by the hand consists of doing good works and righteous deeds. Only Jihad by the sword constitutes Jihad as war.

JIHAD AS WAR

Islam is a religion of peace, but not a religion of absolute pacifism. God has granted Muslims permission to fight and to conduct war in certain well-defined and circumscribed situations.

Those who have been attacked now have permission (to fight back) because they've been wronged, and God can provide them with powerful aid. They're the ones who've been driven from their homes against all right and for no other reason than that they've said, "Our Lord is God." (Qur'an 22:39-40a)

The above statement sets certain conditions that must be met for Muslims to wage war, i.e., Muslims may fight a defensive war against those who have attacked them, provided that in being attacked the Muslims stand in the right—"permission (to fight back) because they've been wronged." Specifically stated, when Muslims are directly attacked and when they are wronged and made homeless for no other reason than that they are Muslims—"for no other reason than that they've said, 'Our Lord is God',' they are permitted to act in self-defense. This concept of the conditional permissibility of Jihad as an act of self-defense is reiterated in several Qur'anic passages.

Fight in the way of God those who fight you, but don't go beyond the limits (of decency and humane conduct), for God has no love for those who go beyond the limits. (*Qur'an* 2:190)

And shouldn't you fight against people who betray their agreements and plot to drive away the Messenger and who take aggressive action against you first? Are you scared of them? By all rights, you should fear God, if you truly believe. (*Qur'an* 9:13)

It just may be that God will create love between you and your opponents, for God is capable enough (to bring that about), and God is forgiving and merciful. God doesn't forbid you from being kind and fair to those who don't fight you because of your beliefs or drive you from your homes, for God loves the tolerant. God only forbids you from having relationships with those who fought you for your faith and drove you from your homes or aided in your exile. Whoever befriends one of these, then they're wrongdoers. (*Qur'an* 60:7-9)

In the last passage quoted above, Muslims are taught that today's enemy may be tomorrow's friend, that Muslims should be "kind and fair" to those non-Muslims who do not wage war against them, and that war is reserved for fighting against "those who fought you for (your) faith and drove you from your homes or aided in your exile."

And why shouldn't you fight in the cause of God and in the cause of those who, being weak, are mistreated: the men, women and children whose only cry is, "Our Lord! Deliver us from this land whose people are oppressors. Send us someone from You who will protect us, and send us someone from You who will help." (*Qur'an* 4:75)

The above statement of God offers additional permission for Muslims to wage war. However, once again, such permission is not absolute, but is severely conditional. One may fight for the sake of God in fighting for the relief of the suffering of innocent victims. Indeed, Muslims have a religious obligation to ease the suffering of the oppressed and to strive for social justice for "those who, being weak, are mistreated." Justice and humane treatment are the rights of every individual, and it is the duty of Muslims to come to the defense of those who are denied these basic rights.

However, let it be noted that permission to wage war has not been granted for the acquisition of territory, geopolitical advantage, colonial exploitation, ethnic pride, political power, or strictly nationalistic concerns. Likewise, if one is fighting for the sake of one's own advantage or for the advantage of one's family, clan, tribe, ethnic group, or nationality, one is not fighting for the sake of God.

> A man said: "Messenger of God, a man wishes to take part in Jihad in God's path desiring some worldly advantage." The Prophet said: "He will have no reward." The people thought it terrible, and they said to the man: "Go back to the Messenger of God, for you might not have made him understand well." He, therefore, (went and again) said: "Messenger of God, a man wishes to take part in Jihad in God's path desiring some worldly advantage." He replied: "There is no reward for him." They again said to the man: "Return to the Messenger of God." He, therefore, said it to him a third time. He replied: "There is no reward for him." (*Abu Dawud, Hadith* #2510)

There is no reward from God for the person who fights with a desire for "some worldly advantage," even when the cause in which he is fighting is a righteous one. In short, a pure and singular motive to serve God is a precondition for any heavenly reward to accrue to a Muslim soldier who is engaged in combat. If part of the motive is to acquire land, there is no reward. If part of the motive is to establish a nation state, there is no reward.

DO NOT TRANSGRESS LIMITS

Having established that Muslims are permitted to wage Jihad as war only within certain set conditions, it must also be emphasized that strict limitations apply to the nature and conduct of any such warfare.

> Fight in the way of God those who fight you, but don't go beyond the limits (of decency and humane conduct), for God has no love for those who go beyond the limits. (*Qur'an* 2:190)

God says there are "limits" to what is permitted in warfare. Islam does not permit Muslims to kill indiscriminately or excessively during times of war. To kill even one innocent person is to stand before God's judgment in the same position as if one had killed the whole of humanity (*Qur'an* 5:32). There are limits that must not be crossed.

LIMITS AND DESIRE

Firstly, no Muslim is to desire war.

The Messenger of God said: "Do not desire an encounter with the enemy, but when you encounter them, be firm." (*Muslim, Hadith* #4313)

God's Messenger, in one of his military expeditions against the enemy, waited till the sun declined and then he got up among the people, saying, "O people! Do not wish to meet the enemy, and ask God for safety, but when you face the enemy, be patient, and remember that Paradise is under the shades of swords." (*Al-Bukhari*, volume 4, *Hadith* #266)

LIMITS AND SUICIDE

Secondly, no Muslim is to commit suicide during warfare.

The Messenger of God observed (that) he who killed himself with steel (weapon) would be the eternal denizen of the fire of Hell, and he would have that weapon in his hand and would be thrusting that in his stomach forever and ever. He who drank poison and killed himself would sip that in the fire of Hell where he is doomed forever and ever, and he who killed himself by falling from (the top of) a mountain would constantly fall in the fire of Hell and would live there forever and ever. (*Muslim, Hadith* #199)

The Prophet said, "Whoever...commits suicide with a piece of iron will be punished with the same piece of iron in the Hell Fire...A man was inflicted with wounds and he committed suicide, and so God said: 'My slave has caused death on himself hurriedly, so I forbid Paradise for him.'" (*Al-Bukhari*, volume 2, *Hadith* #445)

The above *Ahadith* are general indictments against suicide. However, there are also numerous *Ahadith* that concern a specific person, event, and situation. For example, in *Al-Bukhari* #5:514, the story is related of a seemingly valiant warrior, who was respected by his peers and famed for his fighting prowess. Nonetheless, Prophet Muhammad predicted that the warrior would be among the people of Hell. Disconcerted by the Prophet's statement, one man followed the warrior during the course of a battle, only to discover that the warrior ended up committing suicide by impaling himself on his own sword, apparently in order to escape his wounds and his pain. The warrior's suicide was seen as confirmation, as though such confirmation were needed, of the Prophet's earlier statement regarding the warrior.

LIMITS AND COLLATERAL DAMAGE

Thirdly, within Islam, the killing of women, children, and the aged is specifically and unequivocally prohibited. In short, it is a direct violation of Islam to kill civilian non-combatants.

A woman was found slain in one of the battles of the Messenger of God. The Messenger of God forbade killing women and children. (*Abu Dawud, Hadith* #2662)

The Messenger of God said: "Go in God's name, trusting in God, and adhering to the religion of God's Messenger. Do not kill a decrepit old man, or a young infant, or a child, or a woman. Do not be dishonest about booty, but collect your spoils. Do right and act well, for God loves those who do well." (*Abu Dawud, Hadith* #2608)

The next *Hadith* demonstrates just how stringently the Prophet's prohibition against killing civilian non-combatants is to be maintained. In the following example, a woman began to shout, warning the person about to be attacked and giving away the position of the Muslim attackers. Yet, even in these markedly extenuating circumstances, the absolute prohibition against killing female non-combatants was maintained.

The Messenger of God prohibited those people who killed Ibn Abi Al-Huqaiq from killing women and children. One of them said: "The wife of Ibn Abi Al-Huqaiq shouted out and disclosed our presence, and I raised my sword but, remembering the command of the Messenger of God, restrained myself. Had it not been so, we would have been rid of her also." (*Al-Muwatta, Hadith* #956)

The sum total of the above *Ahadith* demonstrates the strict Islamic prohibition against killing civilian non-combatants during war. Specific examples of this include the prohibition against killing women (even those who are attempting to warn others of an impending attack by Muslim soldiers), the prohibition against killing children, and the prohibition against killing the aged. These are prohibitions that know no temporal boundaries and that are unaffected by contemporary issues, events, and technology. To illustrate the permanent nature of these prohibitions, one needs only to turn to the instructions given by Abu Bakr, the first caliph of Islam.

When Abu Bakr Siddiq sent an army to Syria, he...(said) ..."I instruct you in ten matters. Do not kill women or children, nor the old and infirm. Do not cut fruit-bearing trees. Do not destroy any town. Do not cut the gums of sheep or camels except for purposes of eating. Do not burn date trees nor submerge them. Do not steal from booty, and do not be cowardly." (*Al-Muwatta, Hadith* #958)

A parallel version of the above *Hadith* was recorded by Al-Tabari. According to this *Hadith*, Abu Bakr instructed his army with regard to 10 explicit limitations on its behavior as soldiers of God. The army was forbidden to: (1) commit treachery; (2) deviate from the right path; (3) mutilate dead bodies; (4) kill a child; (5) kill a woman; (6) kill an aged man; (7) harm trees, especially those that bear fruit; (8) burn trees, especially those that bear fruit; (9) slaughter the enemy's livestock, except for reasonable food consumption; and (10) bother monks and religious hermits. The *Musnad* of Ahmad ibn Hanbal also lists a *Hadith* that prohibits killing people in places of worship.

There are two aspects of these latter two *Ahadith* that need to be stressed. Firstly, these two *Ahadith*, by extending the ban against killing the aged, women, and children to a ban on killing or bothering monks and religious hermits, clearly demonstrates that the Prophet's injunction was a general prohibition against killing any and all civilian non-combatants. Secondly, these *Ahadith* also elucidate a prohibition against attacking and disrupting the civilian infrastructure, e.g., Abu Bakr specifically instructed the Muslim army not to slaughter livestock (except for that which was needed to feed the army) and not to damage fruit trees.

Quite obviously, a military attack that slaughters livestock and lays waste to food plants is an attack against the civilian population. Such an attack exposes the civilian population to the risk of malnutrition and eventual starvation. Untold numbers of civilians might become seriously ill or even die if such attacks against the civilian infrastructure were permitted. Within Islam, the solution is simple: it is forbidden to attack the civilian infrastructure in such a way as to risk the civilian population.

LIMITS AND TYPES OF WEAPONS

Fourthly, not only does Islam limit who may be the target of a military attack, it also limits the types of weapons that can be employed. The following *Ahadith* illustrate one of these limits on weaponry.

God's Messenger sent us in a mission and said, "If you find so-and-so and so-and-so, burn both of them with fire." When we intended to depart, God's Messenger said, "I have ordered you to burn so-and-so and so-and-so, and it is none but God Who punishes with fire, so if you find them, kill them." (*Al-Bukhari*, volume 4, *Hadith* #259)

Hamzat Al-Aslami and 'Abdullah b. Mas'ud also narrated that the Prophet prohibited killing by burning with fire (*Abu Dawud* #2667-2668). Given this prohibition, one can see that such weapons of war as flame-throwers, napalm, and incendiary bombs are not permitted by Islam.

LIMITS AND FIRST THINGS FIRST

Fifthly, even in such cases where war is incumbent upon Muslims, war does not become the immediate priority. Other issues may well have precedence over war. In the following *Ahadith*, Prophet Muhammad elucidated some of those issues that may supersede the individual Muslim's obligation to go to war. We begin with a *Hadith* that informs us that certain familial responsibilities take priority over the obligation to go to war, even when that war is justified and necessary.

A man came to the Prophet and said, "O God's Messenger! I have enlisted in the army for such and such military expedition, and my wife is leaving for Hajj." God's Messenger said, "Go back and perform Hajj with your wife." (*Al-Bukhari*, volume 4, *Hadith* #295)

In the above *Hadith*, a Muslim is informed that his higher responsibility is to serve as guardian and chaperone for his wife while she performs the Hajj. This marital responsibility outweighs his responsibility to serve as a soldier in the Muslim army, even in times of justified war. At least with regard to the specifics of the above case, Prophet Muhammad taught that being a good husband is more important within Islam than being a good soldier. However, it is not just in the case of one's wife performing Hajj that marital responsibilities take precedence over going to war. In the following *Hadith*, the Prophet also instructed Muslims to give precedence to caring for a sick spouse over fighting in Jihad as war.

'Uthman did not join the Badr battle because he was married to one of the daughters of God's Messenger, and she was ill. So the Prophet said to him, "You will get a reward and a share (from the war booty) similar to the reward and the share of one who has taken part in the Badr battle." (*Al-Bukhari*, volume 4, *Hadith* #359)

Accompanying one's wife on the Hajj takes precedence over Jihad as war. Likewise, caring for a sick wife takes precedence over serving in a Muslim army during times of war. In addition, other *Ahadith* indicate that the newly married husband is excused from serving with the army during war (Al-Bukhari #4:211; 3:589). Once again, a marital responsibility outweighs the responsibilities of serving with the Muslim army during times of war.

In the following *Hadith*, the Prophet taught that both prayer and filial duty to one's parents have a higher priority than the obligation to fight in a war.

Narrated 'Abdullah bin Mas'ud: "I asked God's Messenger, 'O God's Messenger! What is the best deed?' He replied, 'To offer the prayers at their early stated fixed times.' I asked, 'What is next?' He replied, 'To be good and dutiful to your parents.' I further asked, 'What is next?' He replied, 'To participate in Jihad in God's cause.'" (*Al-Bukhari*, volume 4, *Hadith* #41)

Lest anyone doubt that the Prophet explicitly ranked filial duty to one's parents as being a higher good than engaging in Jihad as war, the following two *Ahadith* should end all such doubts.

A man came to the Prophet asking his permission to take part in Jihad (as war). The Prophet asked him, "Are your parents alive?" He replied in the affirmative. The Prophet said to him, "Then exert yourself in their service." (*Al-Bukhari*, volume 4, *Hadith* #248)

A man emigrated to the Messenger of God from the Yemen (intending to participate in Jihad as war). He asked (him): "Have you anyone (of your relatives) in the Yemen?" He replied: "My parents." He asked: "Did they permit you (to participate in war)?" He replied: "No." He said: "Go back to them and ask for their permission. If they permit you, then fight (in the path of God); otherwise be devoted to them." (*Abu Dawud, Hadith* #2524)

LIMITS AND SISTERS IN COMBAT

Sixthly, the Prophet prohibited the use of women as combatants in war. According to the following *Hadith*, 'Aisha narrated that the Prophet taught that women were to make the Hajj pilgrimage and that this was the manner in which they were to exert (Jihad) themselves for God. They were not to serve as combatants in the army.

> Narrated 'Aisha, the mother of the faithful believers: "I requested the Prophet to permit me to participate in Jihad, but he said, 'Your Jihad is the performance of Hajj'." (*Al-Bukhari*, volume 4, *Hadith* #127)

While Muslim women are not to serve as actual combatants in war, several *Ahadith* demonstrate that Muslim women are permitted to give humanitarian and medical care to those men who are fighting in or who have been injured in Jihad as war. Al-Bukhari #4:131-134, Muslim #4453-4456, and Abu Dawud #2525 list the following wartime activities that are permitted to Muslim women: giving water to combatants, providing medical care to wounded combatants, and removing slain and wounded combatants from the battlefield.

LIMITS AND PRISONERS OF WAR

Seventhly, Islam prescribes the humanitarian treatment of prisoners of war. Approximately 1,300 years before the Geneva Conventions were ratified, Prophet Muhammad prohibited the killing of captive members of the enemy.

> Ibn Ti'li said: "We fought along with 'Abd Al-Rahman b. Khalid b. Al-Walid. Four infidels from the enemy were brought to him. He commanded about them, and they were killed in confinement....When Abu Ayyub Al-Ansari was informed about it, he said: 'I heard the Messenger of God prohibiting to kill in confinement. By Him in Whose hands my soul is, if there were a hen, I would not kill it in confinement.'" (*Abu Dawud, Hadith* #2681)

However, Islam goes beyond merely prohibiting the killing of prisoners of war. Islam also prescribes that prisoners of war be treated humanely and that their basic needs be met. This is illustrated by the following Hadith, in which the Prophet saw to the clothing needs of a prisoner of war, Al-'Abbas, who also happened to be the Prophet's uncle.

> When it was the day (of the Battle) of Badr, prisoners of war were brought, including Al-'Abbas, who was undressed. The Prophet looked for a shirt for him. It was found that the shirt of 'Abdullah bin Ubai would do, so the Prophet let him wear it. That was the reason why the Prophet took off and gave his own shirt to 'Abdullah." (*Al-Bukhari*, volume 4, *Hadith* #252)

SUMMARY AND CONCLUSIONS

In summary, the Muslim community's right to conduct Jihad as war is highly conditional. It may fight a *defensive* war against those who have attacked it, provided that the Muslim community is an innocent victim of that attack. However, it then must grant asylum and safe conduct to anyone who lays down his arms (*Qur'an 9:6*). If the Muslim community is not an innocent victim, if it or some part of it actually stands in the wrong, then it is incumbent upon it to make amends for the initial wrong committed by it or its members. The Muslim community may also wage Jihad as war to correct grievous social injustice and wrongs that have been and are being perpetrated against otherwise defenseless individuals. In other words, as a last resort after having spoken "a word of justice to an oppressive ruler" (*Abu Dawud, Hadith* #4330), Muslims may engage in war to alleviate the suffering of the oppressed.

Even when the conditions have been met that would allow Muslims to conduct Jihad as war, Islam prescribes severe and stringent limits on what sort of warfare is permissible. A Muslim must not desire war and must not wish to engage the enemy. A Muslim is prohibited from committing suicide, whether as an act of war or otherwise. A Muslim may not kill or injure civilian non-combatants and must not destroy the civilian infrastructure in a way that eventually causes significant injury or death to civilians. A Muslim is prohibited from mutilating the dead. A Muslim is forbidden to use certain types of weapons, e.g., the use of flame-throwers, napalm, and incendiary bombs to burn others is strictly prohibited. A Muslim must realize and accept that he has certain familial obligations that outweigh his responsibilities to pick up arms, including specified marital obligations and filial duties. A Muslim woman is not to be a combatant in any war, however permissible that war may be. However, she may perform various non-combatant duties, such as caring for the wounded, removing bodies from the battlefield, giving food and drink to soldiers, etc. A Muslim must treat all prisoners of war in a humane manner.

Chapter Six

ISLAM AS A CHAMPION
OF WOMEMN'S RIGHTS

EQUALITY OF THE SEXES

IN CREATION

The *Qur'an* stresses the equality of the sexes in creation by noting that the original man and woman were created from a single soul and that men are women are "equally from each other." Furthermore, Prophet Muhammad emphasized that women are the twin-halves of men (*Musnad* of Ahmad ibn Hanbal). (Of note, the Arabic word for soul is feminine, and the feminine form is carried over into the following translations of the *Qur'an*.)

All you people! Be mindful of your Lord Who created you from a single soul and from her (He) created her mate. From these two were raised all the multitudes of men and women (all over the world). (*Qur'an* 4:1a)

He's the One Who created you from a single soul, and He made from it her mate, so she could dwell with her (husband as a family). (*Qur'an* 7:189a)

...male or female, for you're equally from each other." (*Qur'an* 3:195a)

IN SOCIETY

The equality of the sexes championed by Islam also applies in human society. Thus, the *Qur'an* enjoins that men and women are "protectors of one another," that men and women have their "mutual (rights)" through God, and that women "have rights just as (men) do in all fairness."

The believers, both male and female, are the close protectors of one another. They command what is recognized (as good) and forbid what is unfamiliar (to God's way of life). (*Qur'an* 9:71a)

All you people! Be mindful of your Lord Who created you from a single soul and from her (He) created her mate. From these two were raised all the multitudes of men and women (all over the world). Be mindful of God, the One in Whose name you demand your mutual (rights), and (have respect for women from whose) wombs (you are all born), for God is certainly observing you. (*Qur'an* 4:1)

(Remember that women) have rights, just as (men) do in all fairness, though men have been given an edge over them, and God is powerful and wise. (*Qur'an* 2:228b)

With regard to the last quoted statement that men have been given an edge over women, this refers to innate physical differences between the sexes and to certain economic advantages and responsibilities that fall to men. As a group, men tend to have greater physical strength and speed than women, thus giving them an edge over women in certain areas. Further, as men do not bear children, they have certain advantages when it comes to surviving and to the ability to do strenuous labor without interruption during the late stages of pregnancy. The more primitive the society, the more important those physical advantages become for survival. In modern, technological societies, that edge becomes miniscule. Additionally, in Islam, men have certain economic responsibilities and liabilities that women do not have, a topic that will be developed more fully later.

IN RELIGION

Not only does Islam prescribe equality of the sexes in creation and in society, but also in religion. Good works, righteousness, humbleness, charity, fasting, guarding of chastity, and giving praise to God are prescribed for both men and women. Furthermore, with regard to such behavior, God has promised that He will reward the sexes equally.

Their Lord has accepted them (and will comfort them by) saying, "I'll never let the efforts of any of you who made an effort (on behalf of God) become lost, be he male or female, for you're equally from each other." (*Qur'an* 3:195a)

Whether they're male or female, whoever does what's morally right and has faith will enter the Garden, and not the least bit of injustice will be done to them. (*Qur'an* 4:124)

Whoever does what's morally right, whether male or female, and has faith, We're going to give him a new life that's a life of purity. We're going to reward them according to the best of their deeds. (*Qur'an* 16:97)

For men and women who have surrendered (their wills to God), for men and women who believe, for men and women who are devout, for men and women who are honest, for men and women who are patient, for men and women who are humble, for men and women who donate to charity, for men and women who fast, for men and women who guard their sexuality, and for men and women who remember God often—for them God has prepared forgiveness and a great reward. (*Qur'an* 33:35)

Furthermore, men and women have the same religious responsibilities to pray, practice charity, and obey God. God's mercy showers down on both men and women, and both sexes stand to inherit eternal bliss.

The believers, both male and female, are the close protectors of one another. They command what is recognized (as good) and forbid what is unfamiliar (to God's way of life). They establish prayer, give in charity, and obey God and His Messenger. God will pour His mercy down upon them, for God is powerful and wise. God has made a promise to the believers, both male and female, of gardens beneath which rivers flow in which to dwell, and beautiful mansions in everlasting gardens of delight. However, the greatest delight of all is to please God, and that's also the greatest success. (*Qur'an* 9:71-72)

THE RIGHTS OF WOMEN

As previously noted, the *Qur'an* enjoins that men and women have their "mutual (rights)" through God and that women "have rights just as (men) do in all fairness." This was reiterated by Prophet Muhammad during his Farewell Sermon when he said:

O people! Fear God concerning women. Verily you have taken them on the security of God and have made their persons lawful unto you by words of God! Verily, you have certain rights over your women, and your women have certain rights over you.

So, what are some of those specific rights that women have?

THE RIGHT TO OWN PROPERTY AND TO WORK

Prior to the 19th century, women basically had no right to own property or to earn an income. The marked exception to this sorry state of affairs has always been Islam, which guaranteed women the right to own property and assets, to work, to earn their own money in suitable employment, etc. The *Qur'an* specifically states that women have the right to own property in that they have "a share of what they earn."

For men there is a share of what they earn, and for women there is a share of
what they earn. (Qur'an 4:32b)

In considering the above verse, it should be noted that whatever income a Muslim
woman earns is strictly her own money. Thus, the money earned by a Muslim woman who
is married and has a family is not family income, but it is strictly the income of the woman
who earns it. It is her money, not her family's. She can do with her money whatever she
wishes and is not in anyway obliged to help support the family with her income and assets.
The financial support of the family lies with the husband and father. Furthermore, in the
case of a Muslim woman who is not married, her basic sustenance and living requirements
are the responsibility of her nearest male relative, and once again her income and assets
belong to her alone.

As an additional consideration regarding a woman's right to work and accumulate
her own property and assets, one notes that Khadijah, Prophet Muhammad's first wife,
was a wealthy businesswoman who ran a successful caravan and international trade
business. In fact, prior to their marriage, Prophet Muhammad actually worked for
Khadijah. In addition, Sawdah, another of Prophet Muhammad's wives, worked as a skilled
tanner of animal skins.

THE RIGHT TO INHERIT

Because women in most parts of the world could not own property prior to the 19th
century, they also could not inherit. However, the following verses from the Qur'an
demonstrate that since the seventh century, Islam has insured that women inherit from
their parents, husbands, children, and siblings.

Both men and women have a share in (the estates) that their parents and
nearest relatives leave behind, and whether it's a little or a lot, there's a calculated
share. (Qur'an 4:7)

God Himself gives you the following directions about your children's (inheritance): the male shall receive a portion equal to what's given to two females. If
there are only females, two or more, then their share is two-thirds of the estate;
if only one, her share is half. For parents, a sixth share of the inheritance to
each, if the deceased left children. If the deceased left no children and his
parents are the only heirs, then the mother gets a third, unless the deceased
left brothers, for in that case the mother will get a sixth. (These distributions

will be apportioned only) after the payment of any obligations and debts. You don't know whether your parents or your children are more deserving (of their share), so (accept) these as the settled amounts that are ordained by God, for God is knowing and wise. (Men), in what your wives leave, your share is half if they left no children. If they left children, then you'll receive a fourth, after the payment of any loans and debts. In what you leave, the share (of your widows) is a fourth, if you left no children, but if you left children, then your widows will get an eighth, after the payment of any obligations and debts. If the person whose inheritance is in question has left neither parents nor children, but has left a single brother or sister, then that sibling will get a sixth of the estate; but if there are more siblings, then they will split a third (of the estate among themselves), after the payment of any obligations and debts, so that no loss is caused to any. This is God's decision, and God is knowing and forbearing. (*Qur'an* 4:11-12)

Those (husbands) who leave widows behind them should provide for them (in their will at least) a year's expenses and a place to stay. (*Qur'an* 2:240a)

While some might object that a woman's inheritance is typically half that of a man's, it must be remembered that in Islam the man has all the financial responsibilities of maintaining a family, any unmarried women that are his next of kin, including the woman who may be inheriting alongside of him, etc. In contrast, the woman is free of all such responsibilities, including the responsibility of providing for her own housing, clothing, and sustenance.

Men are responsible for the welfare of women since God has given some (of you) more wherewithal than others, and because they must spend of their wealth (to maintain the family). (*Qur'an* 4:34a)

Thus, while the man's inheritance is really an inheritance by his family, the woman's inheritance is strictly her own. Seen from this perspective, it might even be argued that the woman's strictly personal inheritance is actually larger than that of the man's.

THE RIGHT TO OWNERSHIP OF THE MARRIAGE DOWRY

The *Qur'an* repeatedly stresses that a dowry must be paid by the groom to the bride. This dowry becomes the bride's property and is under her control and direction.

Give women their rightful dowries in the spirit of an honest gift. (*Qur'an* 4:4a)

...all other (women) are lawful (to marry), provided you court them with gifts from your property, desiring chastity and not lust. Since you gain benefits from them, give them their (marriage gifts) as you're required. (*Qur'an* 4:24b)

(With regards to marriage, you're allowed to marry) virtuous believing women, and (you may also marry) virtuous women from among those who received scripture before your time, but only if you give them their required marriage gifts and only if you desire decency and not lustful behavior or secret affairs. (*Qur'an* 5:5b)

...there will be no blame if you (believing men seek to) marry (such women) after offering them a marriage gift. (*Qur'an* 60:10b)

Furthermore, even in the case of subsequent divorce, no matter how large a dowry has been paid, Islam maintains that the dowry remains the woman's property.

However, if you decide to take one wife in place of another, even if you've given the first one a huge mound of gold as a marriage gift, don't take the least bit of it back. (*Qur'an* 4:20-21)

THE RIGHT TO MARITAL CHOICE

Islam prohibited the involuntary marriage of women, insisted that the consent of a woman was needed before any marriage could transpire, and specifically prohibited marriage in which a man "inherits" from a male relative a wife against her will.

All you who believe! You're not allowed to inherit women against their will... (*Qur'an* 4:19a)

God's Messenger said: "It is essential to have the consent of a virgin (for the marriage)." (*Al-Bukhari*, volume 9, *Hadith* #101)

God's Messenger said: "A woman without a husband must not be married until she is consulted, and a virgin must not be married until her permission is sought." (*Muslim, Hadith* #3303)

God's Messenger said: "A woman who has been previously married has more right to her person than her guardian, and a virgin should also be consulted (about her future marriage)..." (*Muslim, Hadith* #3307)

Having established that there is no involuntary marriage in Islam, it is instructive to turn to the *Qur'an's* teachings on the nature of the marital relationship. In a fitting metaphor, the *Qur'an* teaches that spouses are like garments to each other, offering each other protection and warmth. In daily life, nothing comes closer to a person than his or her own clothing. Thus, nothing is closer to a person than his or her spouse. The *Qur'an* also instructs that within the marital state one should "dwell with them in harmony" and that there should be "love and mercy" between the two spouses. Husbands are specifically enjoined that they should not let their wives "languish," should not infringe upon their wives' control of their dowry, and should "live with them in kindness and goodwill."

They're [your wives are] like a garment, and you're like a garment for them. (*Qur'an* 2:187a)

And among His signs is the fact that He created spouses for you from among your own kind so you can dwell with them in harmony. Indeed, He put love and mercy between you, and there are signs in this for people who think. (*Qur'an* 30:21)

All you who believe! You're not allowed to inherit women against their will, neither should you leave them to languish in the hopes of (forcing them to divorce you) and thus getting back part of the marriage gift that you gave them—except in cases where they're guilty of shameful behavior [adultery]. Therefore, you should live with them in kindness and goodwill. (*Qur'an* 4:19)

Supplementing the Qur'anic instructions regarding the marital state, the following *Hadith* of Prophet Muhammad offers additional assurance as to the status of the wife in a Muslim marriage by noting that the best among Muslim men "are those who behave best towards their wives."

The Prophet said: "The most perfect Muslim in the matter of faith is one who has excellent behavior, and the best among you are those who behave best towards their wives." (*Al-Tirmidhi, Hadith* #278)

THE RIGHT TO DIVORCE

Up until the last century or so, divorce within the Judaeo-Christian tradition was strictly the prerogative of the husband and remains so within Orthodox Judaism to this very day. In contrast, Islam acknowledges the right of both the husband and the wife to initiate divorce proceedings and did so well over a thousand years before the Christian West bestowed this right upon women.

> If a wife fears aggressively defiant behavior from her husband or is afraid he will abandon her, it isn't wrong for them if they arrange a fair settlement between themselves (to mutually alter the stipulations of the marriage contract or initiate a divorce). (Qur'an 4:128)

Further, once a divorce has been initiated, Islam guarantees a whole array of rights possessed by the divorced wife. She is guaranteed her reasonable maintenance, the dowry she received upon marriage, and any gifts that her ex-husband gave to her.

> Divorced women should also be given reasonable maintenance. This is a duty for those who are mindful (of God). (Qur'an 2:241)

> There's no blame on you in divorcing women before the consummation of marriage or the settling of the dowry, as long as (the bride) is compensated with a gift—the rich and poor as they're able. A fair gift is a duty upon those who want to do what's most proper. However, if you divorce (a woman) before the consummation of marriage and after the settling of the dowry, then half of the dowry must be given to her unless she forgives it, or (the groom) in whose hand is the marriage tie chooses (to give her the full dowry). Giving the whole to her is closer to piety, so don't fail to be generous to each other, for God is watching whatever you do. (Qur'an 2:236-237)

> A divorce (pronouncement) can only be (revoked) twice. (After that) they must either (reconcile once and for all) and stay together lovingly, or (they must) end their relationship (in a spirit of) fairness. You (men) are not allowed to take back anything you gave to (your wives), unless both sides fear breaking the rules set by God. If so, then there will be no sin on either of them if she returns something (of her dowry) to be free (of her husband). These are the rules set by God, so don't go beyond them; whoever (goes beyond) the rules set by God, they're truly in the wrong. (Qur'an 2:229)

THE RIGHT TO FREE SPEECH

Within Islam, women have been guaranteed free speech and free expression ever since the seventh-century revelation of the *Qur'an*. Furthermore, women had the right to bring their concerns and complaints directly to the attention of Prophet Muhammad. One such notable example is directly referenced in the *Qur'an*.

> God has heard the appeal of (the woman) who brought her petition to you about her husband. Thus, she's bringing her case to God (for resolution). God has heard what both sides have said, for God listens and observes. (*Qur'an* 58:1)

Additional Qur'anic verses, e.g., *Qur'an* 60:10-12, and several narratives concerning Prophet Muhammad, e.g., *Muslim* #7181 and *Al-Bukhari* #7:197-199, witness to women speaking openly, publicly, and on their own behalf, both to Prophet Muhammad and to the community of Muslim believers. As Prophet Muhammad was the Islamic government during his lifetime, the examples of women approaching him to voice their complaints or to ask for redress constitute the Islamic acknowledgement that women have equal rights with men to petition before the court of law.

THE RIGHT TO AN EDUCATION

Prophet Muhammad established the right of every woman to receive an education and did so over a thousand years before the Christian West finally did so.

> The Messenger of God said: "Search for knowledge is compulsory upon every Muslim male and Muslim female." (*Ibn Majah*)

Of special note, despite all his other duties and responsibilities, Prophet Muhammad was directly involved in providing education for Muslim women. The following illustrates this point, as well as reiterating that Muslim women were free to approach the Prophet directly and to petition him with their grievances and concerns.

> A woman came to God's Messenger and said, "O God's Messenger! Men (only) benefit by your teachings, so please devote to us from (some of) your time a day on which we may come to you so that you may teach us of what God has taught you." God's Messenger said, "Gather on such-and-such a day at such-and-such a place." They gathered and God's Messenger came to them and taught them of what God had taught him. (*Al-Bukhari*, volume 9, *Hadith* #413)

At a time and place in which slavery still existed, Prophet Muhammad strongly encouraged every slave owner to educate his female slaves and to manumit them. He stressed that the education of a female slave and her manumission would lead to additional divine reward for her owner, indicating that it was the pleasure of God that female slaves be educated and freed.

> The Prophet said: "He who has a slave girl and teaches her good manners and improves her education and then manumits and marries her will get a double reward..." (*Al-Bukhari,* volume 3, *Hadith* #723)

As a brief digression and as an additional reflection of Islam's encouragement of the abolition of slavery, the following *Hadith* is noted.

> ...God's Messenger said..."God has created nothing on the face of the earth dearer to Him than emancipation..." (*Al-Tirmidhi, Hadith* #3294)

Not only have Muslim women had the right to an education ever since the early seventh century; they have also taught and been some of Islam's greatest religious scholars. Numerous women were narrators of *Ahadith* and gave legal decisions, thus being teachers of both men and women. Other Muslim women memorized all or a good part of the *Qur'an* and were thus Qur'anic scholars in their own right. Other early Muslim women were renowned for their knowledge in such areas as speech, medicine and surgery, and poetry.

CONCLUSIONS

Contrary to popular misconception, Islam was a champion of women's rights in an era in which women were little more than chattel, being literally owned by their husband or nearest male relative. Within that context and breaking sharply with existing social and religious conventions, Islam proclaimed the equality of the sexes in creation, in society, and in religion. Among those rights Islam specifically guaranteed to women were the rights to own and manage their own property, to inherit, to be the sole beneficiary of their marriage dowry, to choose their marriage partner, to divorce, to exercise free speech, to petition the government in their own behalf, and to obtain an education. Sadly, the so-called Christian West failed to grant all of these rights to women for over 13 centuries after Islam's illustrious example.